Civil Paths to Peace

Report of the Commonwealth Commission on
Respect and Understanding

Amartya Sen (Chairperson)
John Alderdice
Kwame Anthony Appiah
Adrienne Clarkson
Noeleen Heyzer
Kamal Hossain
Elaine Sihoatani Howard
Wangari Muta Maathai
Ralston Nettleford
Joan Rwabyomere
Lucy Turnbull

The Commission is indebted to Shamit Saggar and Sarah Ladbury
for their background papers which greatly assisted their discussions.

Commonwealth Secretariat
Marlborough House
Pall Mall
London SW1Y 5HX
United Kingdom

Published by the Commonwealth Secretariat
Edited by Kimberly Clarke
Designed by KC Gan Designs
Printed by Hobbs the Printers Ltd, Totton, Hampshire

Cover photo credit: KC Gan

Copies of this publication may be obtained from

The Publications Section
Commonwealth Secretariat
Marlborough House
Pall Mall
London SW1Y 5HX
United Kingdom
Tel: +44 (0)20 7747 6534
Fax: +44 (0)20 7839 9081
E-mail: publications@commonwealth.int
Web: www.thecommonwealth.org/publications

A catalogue record for this publication is available from the British Library.

ISBN: 978-0-85092-870-9

Contents

Preface

When I was asked by the Secretary-General to chair this Commonwealth Commission, I felt both privileged and challenged. It has been wonderful for me to work with an extraordinary group of exceptionally astute, informed and far-seeing individuals drawn from many different countries of the Commonwealth, bringing a huge wealth of experience and insight to our meetings and interactions.

We recognised the difficulty as well as the momentous nature of the task that the Secretary-General had given us, in line with the decision taken in the 2005 Commonwealth Heads of Government Meeting, 'to explore initiatives to promote mutual understanding and respect' throughout the Commonwealth. The importance of understanding and respect lies partly in their intrinsic value – indeed they are indispensable parts of good living in peace and harmony with each other – but it also lies in their contribution to restraining and removing the group-based violence and terrorism that have become such pernicious features of the contemporary world.

Acts of terrorism and homicide are, of course, criminal activities calling for effective security measures, and no serious analysis of group violence can fail to begin with that basic understanding. But the analysis cannot end there, since many social, economic and political initiatives can be undertaken to confront and defeat the appeal on which the fomenters of violence and terrorism draw to get active foot soldiers and passive sympathisers. The process of recruitment is a battle for people's minds, making crucial use of turbid sentiments and crude reasoning. Cultivated disrespect of target groups as well as engineered misunderstanding of the ways of the world are integral parts of the process of instigating and sustaining violence. This is why the battle against terrorism and group violence has to go much beyond policing criminal activities and confronting military challenges – important though they are.

This report is particularly concerned with what we have called 'civil paths to peace'. The ways and means of pursuing these civil – in contrast with military – routes include a great many instruments, varying from intellectual confrontation of confused and flammable readings of the world (such as unexamined beliefs in the alleged inevitability of a clash between distinct 'civilisations') to institutional changes – governmental and others – that could make it easier for different groups of people to see each other as human beings with a variety of concerns and affiliations that need not be constantly at loggerheads with each other. There are also institutional pitfalls of which we have to be aware, for example a single-minded concentration on expanding the dialogue between religious groups may seriously undermine other civil engagements linked with language, literature, cultural functions, social interactions and political commitments that help to resist the exploitation of religious differences which begins by downplaying other affiliations. The battle for people's minds cannot be won on the basis of a seriously incomplete understanding of the wealth of social differences that make individual human beings richly diverse in distinct ways, rather than being lined up on opposite sides of one gigantic division – religious, racial, national, or whatever.

If the institutional changes needed for pursuing civil paths to peace call for clarity of thought, they also demand organised policies, programmes and initiatives with adequate reach. We have to understand, on the one hand, the role of economic inequalities, social humiliations and political disenfranchisement in generating disrespect and hostility, but we also have to take the concrete steps that are needed for making the hard and often exacting changes in the way the world is organised, in order to remove, to the extent possible, the deeper sources of hostility. Through investigating the linkages between deprivations – past and present – and the fomentation of disaffection, we have tried to identify the central concerns that could usefully guide institutional changes initiated by the respective governments, individually and jointly. But the civil paths to peace are not confined to governmental activities only, since the cultivation of disrespect and hostility can also be resisted by the working of the media, of political processes, of educational activities and other means of generating mutual understanding. We have also identified specific areas of concentration that can sensibly have priority in what we call 'the way forward', and we hope that this will be followed up by an action programme to be developed by the Commonwealth Secretary-General in consultation with member governments on particular policy recommendations.

Central to our work has been the Commonwealth's traditional approach of using multilateralism, making the best possible use of dialogue and discussion. Most members of this Commission shared the conviction that efforts to overcome the scourge of terrorism and group violence in the world could have gone much better had a more multilateral approach been used. But since there is no merit in finger pointing, we have concentrated instead on what can be done here and now to help make the world a more peaceful place than it currently is.

We have argued that being guided by the Commonwealth's multilateral tradition has enormous benefits to offer for all Commonwealth countries, and even beyond our borders. We live in an era of overwhelming global interdependence, and the Commonwealth has duties not only to itself, but also to the world as a whole. We have taken the liberty of discussing not only what we can do for ourselves, but also what we can present to others who share this earth with us, and on whom our own security and peace will, in turn, also depend. In this sense, the report is a modest attempt to present a Commonwealth-based understanding of the civil demands for world peace.

Amartya Sen
Cambridge, 9 August, 2007

Letter of Presentation

8 August, 2007

HE Rt Hon. Donald C McKinnon
Commonwealth Secretary-General
Marlborough House
London SW1Y 5HX

Dear Secretary-General,

We feel very privileged by your decision to appoint us as members of this Commonwealth Commission on Respect and Understanding. The mandate for our work was given at the meeting of the Commonwealth Heads of Government (CHOGM) in Malta in 2005, and we have prepared this report for you for presentation at the next meeting of CHOGM in Kampala, Uganda, in November 2007. We have worked as individual members from Commonwealth countries, and not as representatives of any government or any non-governmental organisation.

We have tried to explore and investigate the content and relevance of respect and understanding between different communities and groups, including faith groups, and the wide-ranging impact of these attitudes for harmonious and flourishing lives within Commonwealth countries. We have paid particular attention to the way group-based violence and terrorism often draw on incitement based on disrespect for each other and misunderstandings of the way the world works. We have also discussed how these evils can be confronted through civil routes, making greater use of the social rewards of mutual respect and fuller understanding.

Indeed, given the prevalence of group-based violence today and the way it tends to ruin human lives and damage peaceful communities, we have focused particularly on the constructive contributions of civil paths to peace in preventing violence and in promoting peace, based on the powerful relevance of respect and understanding. The policies we have discussed are, of course, primarily for possible use in Commonwealth countries, but we believe they may have wider use as well.

Our work has been much assisted by the helpful contributions of our Consultants, Professor Shamit Saggar and Dr Sarah Ladbury, and we are very grateful to them.

We would also like to take this opportunity to note the wonderful co-operation and assistance we have received from the Secretariat, particularly from Alexandra Jones, Daisy Cooper and Matthew Neuhaus. Doing this work satisfactorily within the strict limits of a relatively short time would have been impossible without their help. We would like to thank them.

Finally, we would, of course, like to express our gratitude to you for giving us the opportunity to work on this important problem and for guiding the inquiry through your visionary initiation. We very much hope that the CHOGM will find the Report useful for its deliberation.

Yours sincerely,

Amartya Sen

John Alderdice

Kwame Anthony Appiah

Adrienne Clarkson

Noeleen Heyzer

Kamal Hossain

Elaine Sihoatani Howard

Wangari Muta Maathai

Ralston Nettleford

Joan Rwabyomere

Lucy Turnbull

Executive Summary

This report, which contains the analyses and findings of the Commonwealth Commission on Respect and Understanding, has been guided by the need to develop policy recommendations for Commonwealth Heads of Government, informed by a clear appreciation of the importance and reach of the underlying concepts that give the Commission its name. This report is, thus, both about recommendations of policies to be pursued and about the ways in which policy thinking has to adapt to the realities of the world in which we live. If the cultivation of respect and understanding is both important in itself and consequential in reducing violence and terrorism in the world, the link between the two lies in the understanding that cultivated violence is generated through fomenting disrespect and fostering confrontational misunderstandings. While the report discusses various policy directions as well as particular policy measures, the Commission has requested the Secretary-General to follow up with further specifications for an action programme in consultation with the respective governments.

The Commission was established in response to the decision at the 2005 Commonwealth Heads of Government Meeting (CHOGM) to request the Commonwealth Secretary-General 'to explore initiatives to promote mutual understanding and respect among all faiths and communities in the Commonwealth'. The Commission, appointed by the Secretary-General and comprising eleven experts from a wide range of disciplines and professional backgrounds, met twice in 2006–07 to prepare its report, and also had extensive correspondence and interchange of ideas and suggestions.

With a third of the world's population, the Commonwealth is home to rich and poor, young and old, and people of every colour and creed. It is also an organisation that strives hard to make democracy a way of life. Its composition is inclusive of all political and economic groupings – its 53 members come from every geographical region, represent every stage of development, and include people from all the major religions.

The shared history and traditions of Commonwealth members has yielded administrative, educational and legal lessons that provide fertile ground for the exchange of ideas and best practice. The Commonwealth has used these to good effect, particularly in its support for the poorest and the most marginalised – women, young people, indigenous groups, and the rural poor – particularly those in least-developed countries, including those in small island states.

The Commission believes that the response to confrontational problems should be rooted in the Commonwealth's agreed fundamental emphasis on human rights, liberties, democratic societies, gender equality, the rule of law and a political culture that promotes transparency, accountability and economic development. It is also important to appreciate that the Commonwealth is not just a family of nations; it is also a family of peoples. Furthermore, the Commonwealth provides a shared forum in which governments and civil society meet as partners and as equals. With over 85 pan-Commonwealth professional associations and civil society organisations, the Commonwealth family connects through institutional as well as personal links, and operates through cultural as well as political, social and economic affiliations.

Drawing on the participation of and consultation with its civil society partners, the Commonwealth makes decisions on the basis of negotiation, dialogue, precedent and consensus. This so-called 'Commonwealth approach' of working ensures that members respect each other and try to understand, as fully as possible, the points of view of others. It is to this that the great leader of our time – and former President of South Africa – Nelson Mandela referred in 1994 when he argued that 'the Commonwealth makes the world safe for diversity'.

The need for new thinking about the conflicts in the world

Cultural – indeed 'civilisational' – explanations of world conflict have acquired much popularity recently, to some extent inspired by Samuel Huntington's thesis on the inevitability of 'the clash of civilisations'. That thesis has gained further popularity since the terrible events of 9/11. There has been much discussion about what appears to be an irreconcilable divide between the values of 'us' and 'them' – most notably between the 'West and the rest', between Muslims and non-Muslims. While many have argued, both before and after 9/11, that culture is neither the defining nor the only fault line over which people conflict, the question of how to address the many root causes of conflict has gained a new urgency.

This report has particularly focused on the issues of terrorism, extremism, conflict and violence, for they are much in ascendancy in the contemporary world and afflict the Commonwealth countries as well as the rest of the world. The report investigates the different ways in which such conflicts and violence emerge and are sustained and enlarged. While the cultural influences are among the forces that can contribute to disrespect, misunderstanding and violence, they are not the only causal factors, nor are they immutable or irresistible. Indeed, much can be done to prevent the violence that may be thrust on us by promoters of belligerent agendas. For this we need a departure from old ways of thinking about the centrality and the alleged inviolability of cultural confrontations.

The focus can be put instead on understanding the mechanisms through which violence is cultivated through advocacy and recruitment, and on the pre-existing inequalities, deprivations and humiliations on which those advocacies draw. These diagnoses also clear the way for methods of countering fostered disaffection and violence. In various chapters the different connections are explored and examined to yield general policy recommendations.

Inequality, grievance and history

Beginning with the connection between respect and understanding, on the one hand, and disquiet, disaffection and violence, on the other (Chapter 1), the report explores the various ways through which violence is generated and sometimes wilfully nurtured (Chapter 2).

The role of poverty and inequality in fostering disquiet and hatred, and violence in particular, call for some sophistication of analysis, since the connections are not by any means mechanical and invariant. And yet there are connections, which are discussed in the report (Chapter 3). In addition to manifest inequality, the psychological dimensions of humiliation also demand some depth of analysis.

The history of the world matters to contemporary problems, since the effects of past maltreatment and humiliation can last for a very long time (Chapter 4). The civil paths must, therefore, include addressing past as well as present humiliations. The connections over time, for example through colonial history, are important to understand to appreciate the roots of the actual continuation of inequality and the perceptions of injustice that are seen as being meted out to less privileged parts of humanity. Sometimes the sources of a sense of iniquity and humiliation are real, and they call for remedying (the Scarman Report chaired by Lord Scarman in 1982 is cited here as a good example of policy recommendations following from visionary but detailed diagnoses). When, as is sometimes the case, the confrontational perceptions are exaggerated by confusion (or magnified through extremist instigation), those misapprehensions should still have to be addressed through civil means, with good use of discussion, open scrutiny and a willingness on the part of others to listen to complaints and grievances. The outcomes of these changes would have to be periodically evaluated, in a systematic way, since complex and long-standing problems are not easily eradicated.

Participation, the media and education

If participation is an important part of a suitably multilateral approach to world peace (following the so-called Commonwealth approach), the critical role of political participation within the borders of a country can hardly be over-emphasised (Chapter 5). Attention has to be paid to the reach of the forums for discussion, from central to local, and to ensure that deprived persons are not excluded from the opportunity of joining in and voicing their questions and concerns.

Even though some champions of what they call 'multiculturalism' have shown great hostility to the idea of a national identity, there is nothing in that political concept that reduces the relevance of culture, or religion, or language, in their own respective domains. Indeed, a national identity can be used to give each person an acknowledged equality in political participation, irrespective of religion, race, caste, dialect, or community, or – for that matter – their date of immigration (when that is an issue).

The development of civil society is another area to which special attention has to be paid. A variety of groupings, based on different affiliations, need encouragement and support: the diversity of associations helps to bring neglected concerns to public attention. Governments and civil society organisations have to ensure that those who are consulted are representative of widely held sentiments that can be fairly attributed to the respective groups. Vocal but peaceful political participation can then have the dual role of (1) leading to a more informed making of public policy, and (2) removing discontent about not being heard, which can ultimately contribute to rage and violence.

The Commission believes it is particularly important to pay special attention to women's political participation, since this is often seriously neglected. In this field, the Commonwealth has quite a wealth of initiatives and experiences (some of which the report has discussed), and the different countries can benefit from the experiences of each other.

The Commission submits that it is extremely important to see the role of an unrestrained and flourishing media in helping political participation and dialogue, allowing grievances to be aired and addressed, and facilitating the hearing that public appreciation and complaints should receive (Chapter 6). More specifically the media, encouraged by governments and civil society, can convey a more constructive approach to promoting understanding; tackle causes of grievance and humiliation that underlie the appeal of extremist and instigating messages; help transcend warring boundaries and promote understanding; and develop a fuller understanding of international issues. The Commission emphasises the importance of supporting the media in their constructive efforts – from the operation of training institutions to the actual day-to-day practice of responsible journalism.

The Commission does, of course, recognise that media portrayals can sometimes exacerbate a narrative of oppositional forces, and strengthen, rather than weaken, grievance and disaffection. The media can also, often enough, oversimplify the complexity of current problems. These dangers are there and have to be guarded against (the restraint should come primarily from the internal discipline of good journalism), but they do not, in any way, reduce the importance of the constructive role of the media in giving people more information and more understanding of each other, and also in making them more equipped to deal with potential sources of tension.

Education and young people

The Commission argues that it would be hard to exaggerate the importance of non-sectarian and non-parochial education that expands, rather than reduces, the reach of understanding and reason (Chapter 7). The Commission believes that governments should, as a matter of urgency, give priority to the necessary investment for the universal reach of well-grounded basic education. Inequality in the distribution of education shapes the incidence of exclusion, which is a source of unfairness in itself and can also be a prelude to hostility.

Educational content is crucially linked with the promotion of respect and understanding – or the opposite. The educational curriculum is central in embodying and communicating values and messages about the relationships and understandings between and across diverse identity groups related to different systems of partitioning. Knowledge of world history is particularly critical in helping to forge cosmopolitan identities, as is teaching children about the cultural heritage of a range of ethnic, racial, national, tribal and religious communities. Similarly, teaching children about the value and purpose of social cohesion based on mutual equality is another important objective. Well-designed education can also help in the adaptation of immigrants to their host or new home societies.

The interest and involvement of young people are important not only in the process of education, but also for their contribution to the development of a harmonious society. While the attention that their education demands should never be neglected, it would be a mistake to treat young people as mere recipients of the plans for their instruction made by others, rather than seeing them as thinking beings, whose concerns and enthusiasms can powerfully enrich social life.

The Commission also emphasises the particular role of sports in which the young are commonly involved. Sport should be a vocation open to all people, irrespective of ethnicity, religion, gender or economic circumstances. Given social arrangements for special events, sport can become a reality even for those with a disability. Rigorous training and a commitment to winning medals for one's nation can help overcome many perceived divides within that nation. The Commonwealth Games, and since 2000 the Commonwealth Youth Games, are existing institutional features in which an agenda of greater respect and understanding can helpfully find a direct place, in addition to the indirect contribution they automatically make.

Multilateral approaches

The Commission has been much guided by appreciation of the arguments behind the use of multilateral approaches and their convincing track record. Multilateral consultations and interactions can be of pervasive importance and usefulness in determining appropriate means for pursuing peace and security. The Commission attaches great importance to the Commonwealth's role in placing constructive emphasis on the use of a dialogue-based and consensus-building approach, which can better deliver benefits to all, and also deal more effectively with issues of group-based conflict in the world today.

The potential usefulness of this approach is extensive, perhaps even ubiquitous. To consider a particularly difficult case, the Commission strongly recommends that the Commonwealth's efforts in Zimbabwe must not only continue, but must be strengthened. The Commission also believes that the 'Commonwealth approach' of dialogue and consensus-building may have relevance in other parts of the world: the Commonwealth governments could usefully adopt such an approach in Iraq, where there is a huge – and growing – need for greater multilateral engagements; in Afghanistan, where the international community could strengthen the inclusive initiatives (the report discusses this issue in some detail); and in the conflicts involving Israel and Palestine, where the resumption of dialogue and the cultivation of mutual understanding are critically important. The Commission also argues that multilateralism has relevance in fighting injustice at the international level where some regions and countries have not benefited from the restructuring of the world trade system and where they continue to have little influence over decisions taken in this regard.

The Commission suggests that the Commonwealth Secretary-General's Good Offices work should be extended to address grievance internationally. More particularly, the Commission urges the Commonwealth to use its considerable experience to advocate greater use of multilateral approaches in international disputes and confrontations, working with the United Nations and other international organisations.

The reach of civil paths

Civil paths to peace, the Commission argues, are important and can be very effective. Aside from individual policies, some of which have been spelt out in some detail in the report, there is a big general need for understanding the reach and rationale of using civil paths. The need for hard security measures does not in any way reduce the abiding relevance of pursuing the civil routes.

The Commission argues, in particular, that there is a strong need for much more dialogue and discussion on the richness of human identities and the counterproductive nature of placing people in rigidly separated identity-boxes, linked with religion or community (no matter how positively each religion or each community is described). The importance of people's cosmopolitan identity also demands greater recognition than it tends to get, without denying the relevance of other identities that can comfortably co-exist with a global outlook.

At the international level, civil paths will be inescapably linked with multilateral approaches across borders. At the national level, the avoidance of sectarian divisions within a nation can be a very important component of the civil approach to peace, and the positive features of a non-divisive national political identity should get, the Commission argues, a clear and ungrudging recognition. The Secretary-General has agreed to develop a number of initiatives in consultation with Commonwealth Heads and their governments, for which we hope the resources would be forthcoming. These could helpfully build on the Commonwealth's existing work, or complement the priorities of other organisations, including those of the United Nations (such as the recommendations of the UN's Alliance of Civilisations). Such an action programme would be an important and necessary next step to the Commission's report.

Accepting diversity, respecting all human beings, and understanding the richness of perspectives that people have are of great relevance for all the Commonwealth countries, and for our 1.8 billion people. They are also important for the rest of the world. The civil paths to peace are presented here for use both inside the Commonwealth and beyond its boundaries. The Commonwealth has survived and flourished, despite the hostilities associated with past colonial history, through the use of a number of far-sighted guiding principles. The Commission argues that those principles have continuing relevance today for the future of the Commonwealth – and also for the world at large.

Amartya Sen

John Alderdice

Kwame Anthony Appiah

Adrienne Clarkson

Noeleen Heyzer

Kamal Hossain

Elaine Sihoatani Howard

Wangari Muta Maathai

Ralston Nettleford

Joan Rwabyomere

Lucy Turnbull

Chapter 1: Why do respect and understanding matter?

1   Violence has been a lasting feature of human civilisation, and the contemporary world is no exception to the ubiquitous presence of assault and fury. But the world in which we live today is also one of systematic *group* violence, in which religious, or racial, or ethnic, or territorial divisions are used to foment violence and sometimes even genocide. Recurrent acts of targeting and terrorism make life deeply insecure for those on the 'wrong' side of the targeted separating line. Indeed, global violence clustered around systematically cultivated divisions has a huge presence in contemporary life across the world. Advances in science and technology have also increased the potentially catastrophic destruction of such violence and, as 9/11 has shown, not only in the context of nuclear, chemical or biological warfare.

2   The seriousness of global violence has led to many initiatives aimed at defeating it. Military means for trying to secure peace have been widely discussed and have sometimes also been rapidly deployed, with more reasoned and better informed justification in some cases than in others. And yet group violence through systematic instigation is not *only* – perhaps not even *primarily* – a military challenge. It is fostered in our divisive world through capturing people's minds and loyalties, and through exploiting the allegiance of those who are wholly or partly persuaded. The recruits are prodded into joining, directly or indirectly, various movements for promoting violent actions against targeted groups. Much larger numbers of people are influenced but do not take part in any violent activities themselves, contributing instead by generating a political climate in which the most peaceful of people come to tolerate egregious acts of intolerance and brutality, on some hazily perceived grounds of 'just retaliation' or 'self-defence'.

3   Military initiatives can sometimes be of limited use, when they are well informed, well thought through, and well executed, paying attention to the diverse concerns that have to be borne in mind in any use of force. But many interventions have not met these desiderata, and – as we discuss in this report – they typically leave the root causes of violence unaddressed. They can also generate immensely counterproductive results, by creating fresh hostilities and by giving reason to distinct violent groups to join their hands in 'resisting aggression'.

4   In probing deeper into the causal processes that generate violence and into the ways and means of overcoming them, we have to examine how distortions as well as genuine misunderstandings, such as having a sense of being isolated from the 'mainstream' community, can feed extremism and violence. In alleviating the conditions that give rise to a sense of grievance and isolation through civil rather than military initiatives, and in trying to recover the ground that has already been lost, realistic processes of generating better understanding have a huge role to play. The strengthening of respect (in a very

broad sense) for each other must have a critically important place in any plausible agenda for promoting peace.

5   We have to distinguish between respecting persons (including, of course, their right to hold their own views) and indiscriminately 'respecting every doctrine' held by anyone. Respecting people does not demand accepting their points of view, and a consensus to do something jointly, given the views that different people hold, does not demand that there must be unanimity of substantive views of different people.

6   Respect does, however, demand trying to understand the points of view of others and why they are held, and appreciating the shared interest that people of diverse groups have in cultivating common objectives and finding common ground, such as peace and well-being. This approach suggests a variety of practical actions that can contribute to generating resistance to violence through the social means available to us. The civil routes to peace, which this report explores and presents, are based on a basic appreciation of the role of respect and understanding in this very broad – and constructive – sense.

What do we mean by respect and understanding?

7   In everyday life, the term 'respect' is used in a number of ways. Sometimes it refers to the esteem or honour given to senior people in acknowledgement of their greater age or experience. This denotes deference and implies a relationship that is unequal; though a distinction should be made between respect earned (for example through experience) and power taken note of (for example money or position). But in an inter-cultural context, the term 'respect!' is used quite differently – as a demand for rights and equal treatment. Here it is contrasted with disrespect – the experience of being picked upon, discriminated against, or treated in a demeaning way because, for example, of one's race, colour or culture.

8   In the context of the Commonwealth it makes sense to define respect with reference to rights and equal treatment but to broaden it beyond the issue of race so that it refers to a way of treating others, whatever their age, race, gender or other aspects of their identity, with fairness and with dignity. Looked at in this way, the term respect reflects and encapsulates the principles for which the modern Commonwealth stands – human rights, liberties, democracy, gender equality, the rule of law and a political culture that promotes transparency, accountability and economic development.

9   And respect is about acknowledging a common humanity, and a preparedness to treat everyone, no matter how different their world views, with the dignity they deserve because of their humanity. It is as much about how we treat those who occupy lower social positions as it is about how we respond to those who are more senior. There is an important distinction to make between respecting persons (and their right to hold

their own views) and indiscriminately respecting what they believe in or how they behave. We can show respect to others without agreeing with their particular doctrines or their actions.

10 Understanding implies an ability to grasp what someone else is saying in order to get to the heart of what they are trying to communicate. To do this requires a willingness to put aside one's own preconceived notions in order to appreciate their world view. Understanding, therefore, involves the acknowledgement that one's own culture and experience are not the only models for thinking or acting.

11 Like respect, understanding does not necessarily involve agreement with the views or beliefs others hold. A consensus to do something jointly therefore, given the different views that people hold, is not preconditioned by the necessity of any unanimity of view. No-one or nobody should hold a veto that requires subordination of all to a single view or belief.

12 It is also important to understand disrespect and what it is like to be disrespected. Disrespect for an individual or a community can be expressed simply through passive rejection, ignoring their presence and their needs. The poorest people – those marginalised by their poverty, social status, gender or disability – often have the least power to mobilise and make demands. Local services might be high quality but still be delivered in ways that make poor women feel like cattle, or worse. And being a woman might mean that you are all but certain to receive a sub-standard service. Being treated as invisible or irrelevant in a clinic, on a bus, or in a shop is an indication of disrespect. It is equally possible that those who are put in positions of authority can be treated with disrespect, not because of how they have behaved, but simply because they are in authority. Respect should be a characteristic of all our relations.

13 Respect and understanding are intimately connected with human rights expressed in terms of the four great freedoms (from hunger, disease, ignorance and fear) – to which one might add freedom from violent conflict. These freedoms are not attainable in a vacuum. They necessarily require consideration of the nature of basic values that underlie the actions necessary to achieve these freedoms.

Respect and understanding and the Commonwealth

14 Respect and understanding are values at the heart of what we might call the 'Commonwealth approach'. This approach involves a tradition of doing things through dialogue, where everyone has the right to speak, to be heard and to be consulted in coming to a common view. It involves a belief in a shared process and in the ability of people – all people, no matter how diverse – to make use of that process. In essence, it is about seeking a consensus and valuing the process that brought about coming to a common view.

15   The principle of dialogue can be seen as part of respecting each other and wanting to achieve understanding rather than unilateral victory. In practice, dialogue between Commonwealth members has not always involved agreement. Indeed, the approach that has been used could even be described as getting by without an agreed perspective, but *with* some agreed and recognised general principles on how to do things.

16   The Declaration of Commonwealth Principles first agreed in Singapore in 1971, and then reaffirmed in Harare in 1991, reflect the importance given to respect and understanding by Commonwealth countries. These Principles emphasise the human rights of all citizens regardless of gender, race, colour, creed or political belief and the need to absolutely oppose racial prejudice and all forms of racial oppression. They recognise the urgency of economic and social development and the need to progressively remove disparities in living standards to achieve a more equitable international society. They also affirm the importance of active participation by civil society, including by women and young people, through free and democratic processes.

17   Individuals and countries of the Commonwealth have valuable experience in putting respect and understanding into practice, having played catalytic roles in helping to liberate peoples from colonialism and apartheid. The multi-ethnic and multi-religious membership of the Commonwealth embraces a diversity of faiths, cultures and societies that are marked by divisions of rich and poor, powerful and powerless, and of caste and class. The Commonwealth is therefore a microcosm of the challenges being faced in today's conflict-ridden world, but also of the determination to find solutions – not through confrontation, but through an agreement that all parties have the basic right to be fully involved in dialogue processes.

18   There are also established ways of working in the Commonwealth that have proved fundamental in putting respect and understanding into practice. The organisation seeks consensual rather than confrontational debate. It seeks out those principles on which member states can agree – whether on democracy and good governance, human rights, including those of women, or the importance of development and economic justice. It is informal and non-threatening in manner and tends to work behind the scenes in non-public ways.

19   At the same time, the wealth of non-governmental connection in the association, through Commonwealth civil society, works away at the cultural context in which these values have meaning and application, to promote respect and understanding. There are many practical examples of how Commonwealth institutions and societies contribute to a discussion and exchange of views between members of different Commonwealth countries to build respect and understanding, including between young people.[i]

i   RCS 2007. Examples include the Royal Commonwealth Society's 'Commonwealth Essay Competition' (open to all students aged between 8 and 18) and its 'Youth CHOGMs' (a simulation of the Commonwealth Heads of Government Meeting); and, the Commonwealth Policy Studies Unit's 'Commonwealth Clubs in Secondary Schools' project.

20   One of the striking social changes which is currently taking place across the globe is the move from hierarchical structures to networks. We experience this dramatically in the operation of the internet, but this is merely one example of the phenomenon. The Commonwealth has always tried to operate ahead of the game in this regard since it has always operated as a network, and is therefore not only a suitable format for future international relations, but has valuable experience to share with more traditional international and intergovernmental formations.

21   That said, all Commonwealth member countries and organisations recognise the very real challenges that the Commonwealth has faced, and will continue to face, in adhering to a shared set of fundamental principles, living out these values and dealing with situations when these are flouted or abused. Over the years, there have inevitably been divergences in perspective within the Commonwealth, not least in the area of human rights. The openness of discussion and debate has sometimes brought to the surface deep divisions in perspectives that have not been resolved by extensive dialogue.

22   There is very strong support for parliamentary democracy within the Commonwealth – to a great extent inspired by the British experience but also drawing on traditions of debate and discussion in other Commonwealth countries.

23   What behaviour is or is not consistent with Commonwealth principles and values? The basis of the Commonwealth is frank and open discussion with the right of all to speak and to be heard. As a result, denying people the freedom to participate in the public life of their own country will always be in tension with membership of the Commonwealth.[ii]

24   Whilst the Commonwealth does have ways of taking action against unacceptable political behaviour on the part of governments, all efforts are made to keep lines of communication open (for example with countries under suspension). This is to ensure that there remain channels for supporting the efforts of those within a country who are struggling to re-establish democratic practice and respect.

25   In many countries the Commonwealth approach to dialogue has yielded significant and positive results and has even achieved consensus across previously entrenched divisions. South Africa's peaceful transition from apartheid to a modern democracy is a powerful example of the approach in action, not least in ensuring that previous critics of sanctions against a white minority-rule regime were brought around to support a common strategy. Also, as we discuss further in paragraphs 224–226, had greater priority been given to an interactive civil approach after the initial defeat of the Taliban regime in Afghanistan, some of the residual problems there might have been avoided, which have instead resurfaced and grown stronger over the years.

---

ii   Sen 1998.

Why do respect and understanding matter now?

26 Respect and understanding matter now for three important reasons that drive the timeliness of this report:

- Firstly, because of the prevalence and the far-reaching effects of violent conflict in the world today and the apparent persistence of conflict even as, or perhaps because, the world grows more interconnected.

- Secondly, respect and understanding in the world is critical now because of the persistence of terrorism and the fear of terrorism.

- Thirdly, as we have already noted above, our increased technological capacity for destruction through ever-more sophisticated and powerful weapons of war makes the avoidance of human and environmental catastrophe as a result of war a matter of profound urgency.

27 Violence is deeply disturbing and even low-level violence at a community level has enormous impacts. Fear of its continuation may stop people going to work or sending their children to school; relations of trust between neighbours may break down, further isolating vulnerable groups such as the elderly. If the police move in clumsily, or act in a way seen to be partisan, then the risk of violence is likely to increase – with the police also seen as potential perpetrators. In the longer term, violence damages the whole economy – for example, through reducing inward investment, raising the cost of doing business and removing the skills and the savings of those who can afford to move away.

28 Violent conflict also takes a huge toll on the poor and on the prospects for reducing poverty. Of the 34 countries currently furthest from reaching the Millennium Development Goals (MDGs), 22 are in the midst of, or emerging from, violent conflict. The consequences usually fall most heavily on women and children, who make up the majority of displaced people – at times of violent conflict women and girls often experience rape, sexual violence, forced pregnancy, kidnap and abuse.

29 The Commonwealth is not immune to conflicts within and between its member countries. At the end of 2003 nearly half of the 23 armed conflicts between and within states around the world were in Commonwealth countries. The Commonwealth has extensive experience in addressing conflicts, and, more importantly, defusing the tensions that create them.

30 Respect and understanding in the world are critical now because of the persistence of terrorism and the fear of terrorism. Some of the ways in which this is being tackled seem to have the effect of provoking, not reducing, violence and terrorist acts. A new, or at least a complementary approach, is urgently needed.

31   The Commission is persuaded that some of the policy actions taken to protect citizens from further terrorist attacks have been limited in their conceptualisation and in their effectiveness. Because of the importance given by all governments to the threat of terrorism today it is worth setting out our understanding of the limitations of current approaches.

The so-called 'War on Terror'

32   Current approaches to the 'War on Terror' raise many questions on a number of fronts. Most importantly, there has been a tendency to see terrorism as essentially a military or security threat requiring, primarily, a military and security response. Where a military intervention has been tried and there has been an effort to effect democracy by military means, as in the case of Iraq, it has not succeeded either in military terms or in terms of leaders being able to maintain the support for a sustained intervention by their publics at home or internationally. In Afghanistan, where the rationale for intervention was to remove a regime that posed a threat to international peace and security through its extensive support of terrorism, efforts to establish a new democratic constitution – which would have been challenging enough in any circumstances – have been undermined by the diversion of resources to Iraq.

33   World public opinion has taken a dim view of this approach and has raised many questions, not least whether the war on terror itself is helping to sustain feelings of grievance and therefore contributing to the possibility of future attacks, as well as to a higher level of violence in countries like Afghanistan, Pakistan and Iraq. There have been many unintended consequences of adopting the strategy of a 'War on Terror,' not least that aspects of the strategy seem to have further inflamed sentiment across the world. Not surprisingly, there has been a loss of hope and a growing cynicism about a felt loss of the common international values and standards that all nations in principle adhere to.

34   It could be argued that, in Britain and America, attempts at engaging against terrorism through the medium of faith and religion have had, at times, a perverse effect of magnifying the voice of extremist Islamists at a time when the political and civil roles of Muslims in civil society, including in the practice of democracy, need emphasis and much greater support. Faith-based approaches make it more difficult for politically secular Muslims (who do not have any standing, or any great urge, to speak in a faith-based discussion) to speak out against terrorism and violence. Like everyone else, they feel 'voiceless' in the middle of faith-based discussions. Religious extremism has made citizens, whatever their religious affiliation, less capable of taking responsible political action and speaking out against violence. And this tendency has often been strengthened rather than weakened by attempts to combat terrorism through recruiting the religious establishments of various communities to 'the right side', with young people being dismissive of the older religious establishment spokesman when they line up with Western governments. Civil society is currently in need of strengthening with

all the positive resources at our disposal. Whilst religious identities can be used in a very positive way, by for example instilling a moral code and way of living, stressing religious identities over and above other political and social identities can undermine efforts to strengthen civil society and community cohesion. The culturally rich, more nuanced non-religious aspects of pluralism have been downplayed at precisely the wrong moment. This makes it easier for belligerent extremists to gather support and gain a stronger foothold in many countries.

35   There have been other casualties of the strategy of the 'War on Terror'. In countries that have themselves experienced terrorist attacks, greatly enhanced additional surveillance operations and a raft of new counter-terrorism laws have raised questions about the state's ability to uphold the rule of law and individual rights. The difficulty is the balance these new measures and laws must achieve to allow policing and security agencies to find and prosecute suspects for criminal offences, whilst maintaining legal safeguards in the criminal justice system that protect individual freedoms and uphold the rule of law.

36   A major concern is that the strategy of a 'War on Terror' may be helping to increase support for the messages of oppression, humiliation and disrespect that groups involved in terror attacks are putting forward. Where state responses have included extra-judicial measures that allow the government to circumvent national or international law, or if the military response is seen as disproportionate and is interpreted as vengeance, or if the measures proposed to tackle terrorism are seen as simply unworkable then, almost perversely, this can increase public support for the message, if not the methods, of the insurgents. People may abhor the use of terror tactics but nonetheless have some sympathy for those who seem to be subjected to laws which they perceive to be harsh and undemocratic, and as a result show concern for the rights of these people as a means of expressing their opposition to the impacts of counter-terrorism strategies. The public can be antagonised by the adverse impact of official reactive security measures, especially if they are not proportionate. On the one hand, the Commission accepts and endorses the importance of effective security measures for the prevention of violent crime, no matter how generated. The strength of security which we firmly support must not, however, be confused with an image of indiscriminate toughness that gives people a false sense of security.

37   Terror attacks carried out in the name of a particular identity inevitably have the potential to polarise societies. Sadly, counter-terrorism strategies can themselves exacerbate this polarisation. The threat of terrorism following 9/11 fostered particular resentment of perceived migrants in many countries, particularly migrants of Muslim origin.[iii] The response of many Muslims was to retreat from public discourse at exactly the moment that more Muslim voices were needed. When new security measures are imposed quickly

---

iii   UN DESA, 2004, 2.

following a terror attack, without due debate, discussion and sensitivity, this can further divide people at a time when more engagement is what is required.

38   Those communities perceived to share an aspect of their identity with the perpetrators are then particularly vulnerable. Increases in hate-related violent attacks against minorities are extensively documented for all countries that have experienced terrorism. Efforts to protect and reassure minority communities – who often feel acutely vulnerable – that are carried out through community policing strategies and dialogue with community leaders, have greatly helped. But the problem could be better mitigated by a response which simultaneously consults with minorities, community groups and civil society about the short and long-term consequences of all aspects of counter-terrorism action at the same time as taking reasonable, well-conceived and well-communicated security measures, both internal and external.

39   Terrorism is not simply like other forms of political violence. The Commission sees terrorism as a tactic – as well as a crime. It may be used by the left or the right, or by populist or nationalist extremists. It involves the premeditated use of violence to create a climate of fear, but is aimed at a wider target than the immediate victims of the violence. The victims may have symbolic significance but the real target is not the victim. The target is the 'responsible authority', for example a government or a dominant group. The aim of many terrorist groups is to force a reaction – or overreaction – by the responsible authority toward terrorist acts and those who perpetrate them. It is this (over)reaction that makes it possible to cast the government or responsible authority as the greater villain.

40   The 'responsible authority' (or its historic predecessors) is seen as having perpetrated an injustice. Terrorists and their supporters see themselves as righting some terrible wrong, some humiliation, some deep disrespect that has been done to them, their community or their nation by an authoritarian government or state. Terrorists and their supporters believe that they are 'freedom fighters', embarking with great courage and risk to themselves on a heroic task, namely of righting that perceived wrong.

41   Yet the nature of this injustice, the 'terrible wrong' that they aspire to right, is under-explored. There is a disinclination to understand – never mind talk to – those involved because of the means through which their grievances are expressed. The tendency at national level to exclude groups classified as terrorists from the political process, through listing them in Terrorism Acts and Criminal Codes, is the antithesis of a process based on dialogue. Where dialogue is possible, and where the stated aim of terrorists is ending repression and humiliation and having a greater level of inclusion in society and its political processes, then dialogue is essential – as hard as that is to engage in where there is violence and fear. Where it may not be possible is where there is a militant goal to destroy a democratic society or way of life based on the rule of law. In that case, it is essential to create the conditions where there is less capacity for extremists to win the hearts and minds of others to their cause: that can only be done

through creating the perception that it is possible for members of minorities to feel included in society and to have a shared sense of destiny in a common future.

42   Dialogue with groups at the far ends of the political spectrum, or with those that hold views that most people feel are repugnant, is a probing and uncomfortable test for countries that have experienced terrorism. Yet it must be done, or tried, where the objectives of the terrorists do not include the complete destruction of a democratic state governed by the rule of law. Whilst not underestimating the difficulties of the Commonwealth experience, the fundamental truth is that the willingness to listen and engage in dialogue not only helps but is the only way to bring any form of political violence to a sustainable end. It also addresses the criticism that peace is unlikely without addressing justice.

Understanding root causes better requires challenging various cultural theories

43   The tendency to present the causes of conflict or terrorism as having their roots in a clash of civilisations has seized the popular imagination. The Commission believes such cultural theories to be deeply flawed on a conceptual level and deeply divisive in practice.

44   For one thing, separating the world into discrete civilisations assumes that: (a) the millions of individuals classified under each categorisation identify with the persona they are 'given', and (b) there is sufficient homogeneity within each identified group for the categorisation to mean something.

45   Furthermore, these cultural theories have tended to presume that the groups so identified will inevitably clash. The Commission categorically rejects this claim. There is simply no substantial evidence for it. Millions of people may be represented as being either part of 'the Islamic world' or 'the West' (to take two examples of such cultural categories), but neither Muslims nor Westerners think, act or believe as one. Individuals within these hugely differentiated population groups have multiple affiliations, multiple identities. There is as much discrepancy in belief, political position and cultural practices *within* the populations referred to as between them.

46   Being Muslim or Western can never be an overarching identity that determines everything that a person believes in or is prepared to do. It is imperative that world leaders are not seduced into thinking that these categories, representing as they do such a diverse range of peoples, accurately capture the feelings and values of those so categorised, much less that they have the power to 'explain' violence. Reducing people to such categories represents only part of them, rather than the whole persons they are, and fails to recognise the complexity of their diverse affiliations and identities.[iv]

---

iv   On this see Sen 1999, and Sen 2006.

47   Taking up this challenge now is vital: theories such as the 'clash of civilisations' are already widely reflected in the press and have found their way into a range of explanatory frameworks that in turn influence public policy. They will inevitably find their way into classroom discussions and, ultimately, textbooks, thus institutionalising a way of thinking that will indirectly influence young people. For the Commonwealth, it is also important to avoid inadvertent regressions to a divisive mindset.[v]

48   The issues discussed in this report are therefore substantial concerns in their own right across the world. The Commonwealth is no exception in feeling the consequences of greater sensitivity about ethnic and religious identity, and the effects of the failure to tackle grievances.

49   This Report operates within this larger context, which itself is constantly evolving and developing, in part through the work of governments and international organisations, to address underlying issues. Indeed, even with a robust and shared understanding of the problem, it is important that those holding political and economic power implement appropriate remedies to the fullest extent that they are able. This will require additional effort to ensure that:

- The rationales for intervention in particular situations are clear and demonstrable, and are thus more likely to promote consensus (or more near-consensus) about what needs to be done.

- The potential responses are viewed within the framework of various existing Commonwealth and inter-governmental objectives (including ending violent conflict, promoting development, extending democracy, addressing sustainability, tackling extremism and identifying the root causes of radicalisation).

- There are better understandings of emerging challenges, for example through policies aimed at targeting highly disengaged groups who are at risk of sinking into deeper and/or further kinds of alienation.

- Governments in particular appreciate their own limitations and fully recognise the role that others (such as the business and civil society communities) can play. The influence of neighbouring giants or regional superpowers, the mass media and market behaviour may mean that a particular governments' role is limited in any case.

- Important gaps in knowledge and understanding are flagged, in order to establish priorities for follow-up work among practitioners and also among researchers.

50   With the above caveats in mind, it is important still to remember that in many cases there is much more that governments can do to secure greater respect and understanding. This must of course never involve turning a blind eye to gross discrimination and victimisation. It might involve articulating clearly that government itself stands for the principles of respect for individuals as human beings, and that all

---

v   On this see Appiah 2006. See also Appiah 2004, and Sen 2006.

people have the right to be treated fairly and with dignity. Government can also: (a) adopt policies that tackle gross unfairness and injustice, (b) create systems which give citizens and their preferences a strong voice, and (c) acknowledge the role of the international community in shaping universal values and promoting positive change.

51   There are other things that governments can do, in policy-making in many areas, to develop the sorts of connections across groups that are so crucial to avoiding conflict. Even the operation of the military can contribute to this. Armies and police forces provide a crucial mechanism by which people of diverse origins can be brought together in a context that enhances respect and understanding. Most people enter the armed or police forces when young. Their attitudes are still forming. And the military and the police are institutions that, by their nature, must exercise more control over the lives and attitudes of its members than any other government bodies. Strict insistence on non-discrimination, promotion without regard to ethnicity, and the principle that all must be willing to take orders from superiors, whatever their social origin, creates a context in which even those who may enter with discriminatory attitudes can often be persuaded to change them for the better. The approach of the military in dealing with people in the communities in which they work is also vital. More than ever the real military struggle is for the hearts and minds of people rather than simply for control of territory, and this requires a very different set of skills. A serious long-term commitment to sport in multi-ethnic teams can have similar good effects.

52   Social psychologists confirm what common sense suggests: people who work together when young in circumstances of equality and mutual dependence across races, religions and ethnicities, tend to be less prejudiced than those who do not.[vi] Similarly, in the area of employment, integrating government workplaces and enforcing anti-discrimination laws in the private sector can lead to developing cross-group linkages outside the workplace.[vii] In the context of educational policy, encouraging young people not only to study together but to play sports, engage in community activities, make music, and otherwise work together across groups, can have similar beneficial effects. In all these cases – the military, government and private sector employment, and education – there are opportunities to shape policies and develop practical proposals that will encourage respect and understanding.

53   Although others have an important role to play, the role of government in supporting respect and understanding is unique. For one thing, despite obstacles, it is often much better placed to provide standards of equality and equal treatment. Government can also pursue strategic public policy goals to remedy unfairness and injustice. And, of course, properly accountable government is in a position to be answerable for its actions and inactions.

---

vi   Moskos 1986.

vii   Estlund 2003.

Chapter 2: The Nature and Nurture of Violence

The nature of violence

54   Violence is the most recognisable form of disrespect, a very public indicator that respect and understanding have broken down. It takes many forms but it is useful to make two sorts of distinction:

- First, between violence carried out in the course of ordinary crime for personal gain (robbery and the like) and political violence. Our concern is with the second, but the first is also important as robbery itself shows intense disrespect to the person whose property is looted or stolen or whose person is harmed. Nor are ordinary crime and political violence necessarily distinct, the two can merge: the overall cause of the leaders may be political but their supporters and followers may act with a mix of personal motives (looting can be for monetary advantage, acts of atrocity or honour can be carried out to enhance personal status, and organised crime pursued as a way to finance an illegal insurgency or terrorist campaign).

- The second necessary distinction is between violence that is primarily physical and violence that involves no physical contact but can have deep psychological effects. Violence of this sort can manifest itself as a form of intense yet unspoken disregard. The poorest people, those marginalised by their poverty, social status, gender, age or disability, tend to experience this form of 'violent disrespect' most intensely. It is communicated simply through passive rejection of their existence – by being treated as invisible or irrelevant in everyday life. It is often evident where inequalities are endemic and have become institutionalised; unfair treatment then becomes part of the social structure.[viii]

- Physical and psychological violence are often combined. Violence is rarely 'just' a physical attack aimed at causing hurt or pain. It is also an attack on personhood, on the human-ness of others, on an individual, community or institution's sense of self-worth, on identity.

- The rape of women in war is an extreme example of an attack on personhood. Whilst it is a physical act that aims to cause individual women physical and mental pain, it is also a symbolic act that reflects the notion of women as embodiments of national and cultural identity that can be violated through their bodies. Violence against women is, therefore, aimed at destroying the honour and self-respect of the whole group, not alone in the present, but because of the special role of women in bearing the next generation, a destruction of the hopes for the future.

---

viii   For example, dalits (scheduled castes), tribals (scheduled tribes), other castes and Muslims who are poor and disadvantaged face serious levels of exclusion in some South Asian countries in terms of their access to income, education, social services and their participation in political and decision-making processes.

55   Violence of these types, although important in many contexts, and as we have noted frequently symbolic in various respects, has to be distinguished from the violence associated with terrorism. The victims of terrorist attacks may be the terrorist's own community or even his or her own body but the target is authority. Terrorist forms of violence intentionally break basic human codes of conduct, so that by violating all social norms it provokes outrage and cannot be ignored. The motives can be complex: through his or her actions, a terrorist may be trying to force concessions, affect public opinion, or bring attention to their cause. It may even be an act of desperation. But in some cases, there is undeniably a much stronger symbolic aspect: the organisationally 'weak' terrorist group aims, in addition to drawing attention to their own injustice, to provoke the 'strong' authorities into a substantial overreaction that will damage their standing and moral authority both domestically and internationally.

56   Those who are most disadvantaged may even internalise their disadvantage and feel a sense of worthlessness; whilst acutely aware of their position they may be profoundly disempowered by it, particularly if previous attempts to change their status came to nothing. They may endure their situation without protest in case their demand for justice incites worse repression. This form of violence is rarely heralded by loud protest. It is endured by millions the world over as part of the 'normal' order of things.

57   Some of the most entrenched social, economic, political and cultural injustices are endured by women, half the world's population. Young people may also be ignored as they also tend not to be the leaders of their communities or to have a voice in their institutions. They therefore lack the power to shape agendas. Even when their voices are heard they are not always systematically mainstreamed into national debates. Women and young people have to struggle particularly hard to command respect in countries where principles of patriarchy and seniority determine who holds power, and the damage suffered is transmitted inter-generationally. Again, this exclusion is not violence in a physical sense but a violation of their right to be heard and respected, which supplements the iniquity and barbarity of actual physical and sexual violence and abuse against women and young people by men. This is a priority issue in making the world a more just place.

The nurture of violence

58   Political violence is nurtured by psychological as well as physical factors. For violence to be sustained the 'other side' must be seen as not only different but also associated with beliefs or actions felt to be inimical to a way of life or dearly held values. In short, the other side must be seen as a threat. Violence against the other can then be presented as protecting one's own way of life. If violence is seen as a form of self-defence ordinary people are more likely to accept it as morally justified.

59   A first and concerning step on the road to violence is, therefore, the truncating of identities down to a single category. It is not hard to see how this helps to draw potential battle lines. One of the most frequently used means of creating in-group solidarity comes from framing the out-group as threatening, parasitic or worse (a form of 'scapegoating'). Such sentiments take hold by denying the commonality of experience and interest that lies across and between groups. In the case of systematic, organised sectarian violence, this element becomes central to the ability of leaders to rally supporters and target a single common foe.

60   Two observations stand out when contemplating this problem in its severest form:

- The first is that extreme circumstances are hallmarked by a politics that rejects negotiation. That is to say, one side's willingness to discuss and negotiate the shape of the grievance or concern of the other side is completely undermined by their inability to see the other side in terms that are recognisable or have inherent value. The most extreme version, of course, is to portray the other side in non-human terms, thus obviating the need to justify hatred or violence.

- The second observation is that one-dimensional identity is fundamentally flattening in its purpose and in its outcomes. It is designed to deliver an all-powerful lens through which the world is seen, though not required to be understood. Wearers of the lens are provided with a world-view that is sufficiently all encompassing to relegate individual choice to the margins. In extreme conditions, it supplies a plentiful source of nourishment to build and sustain hatred. The odds against mutuality, or interlocking lines of empathy and solidarity, are heavy stacked as a consequence.

Identity politics and its distortion

61   The rise of identity politics of this kind is far from new. Even in modern times, there are no shortages of vivid illustrations of powerful, exclusionary hate-driven identity politics and movements that have denied even the most minimal value to others. National Socialism in Germany in the mid-twentieth century is arguably the most well-documented example. The partition of India in the 1940s was characterised by the same elements, most notably the sudden evaporation – and denial, in many cases – of cross-community links and bonds. And the chapter of African slavery in the New World (to say nothing of the related chapter of indentured labour throughout the European imperial world) from the sixteenth to nineteenth centuries, is a compelling example of the assignment of one racial identity as a means of creating political and cultural dominance.

62   But, even putting these large examples to one side, it is equally important to note a general trend towards the growth of one-dimensional identity politics and fundamentalism. This has been observed both in the developed and developing worlds. As a partial result of (a negative reaction to) globalisation, it has meant that particular kinds of identity-based conflict are now much more rapidly projected in a range of

otherwise quite dissimilar societies. For instance, contentious and campaigning forms of collective identity have emerged in recent years that centre on opposition to the potentially 'homogenising forces of globalisation'. These identities have found it relatively easy to fuse or find common cause with related concerns about the economic domination of global corporations, threats of environmental degradation and failure to tackle perceived regional injustices. Campaigns of opposition to all of these things often converge, and people with very different views campaign together against the authorities who they regard as being 'to blame', though often for quite opposite reasons.

63   One-dimensional identities are particularly nurtured where an overarching value system is put forward to justify the basis for being against each and all of these forces. The narrative of anti-globalisation movements is a simple, ready-made way of supplying such a narrative, and this has had remarkably powerful effects in shaping a sense of common understanding. Given that the dynamics of a globalised economy are far from being perfectly understood, it is clear that this reaction is actually an emotional rather than an intellectual response, with fear being the dominant emotion involved. Nevertheless, a form of single dimension of identity has emerged that has been impressive in appealing to the multiple identities that underpin concern and opposition to various aspects of globalisation. It is striking that a number of anti-globalisation movements have been effective in doing just this.

Faith and identity

64   Faith has always been a particularly powerful force in the construction of identity. Faith is often a force for good; the values of all of the main faiths of the world promote love and understanding, respect and hope, care by the strong for the weak, and societies based on justice, fairness, co-existence and harmony.[ix]

65   The Commonwealth Foundation has recently launched an innovative project examining faith, development and social cohesion. It aims to:

■ encourage debate and advance learning about collaboration between faith-based groupings in addressing development and social issues, and

■ investigate the value and relevance of inter-religious co-operation, and particularly the roles this can play in helping to address development and social issues.

66   This initiative centres on perspectives (mainly drawn from a non-governmental background) on inter-religious co-operation. These are used to stimulate further debate on the scope and potential for inter-religious co-operation for greater social cohesion. It represents a basic building block of mutual respect and understanding across traditional boundaries.

---

ix   Clarke 2006.

67   However, faith has also been used throughout history to promote the interests of those with destructive aims. As a legitimising discourse for violence, faith has an advantage over purely political ideologies because of its ability to justify, inspire, empower – and not be proved wrong. This is due to the transcendental nature of belief ('fighting injustice is God's will'), the inspiration of religious hope ('God will fulfil His promises') and the centrality of faith ('no matter how bad things get, this is the Right Way'). Fearful believers may come to accept, if only inadvertently, a 'politically activist theology of violence', which usually means reconciling 'a single, simultaneously loving and violent God'.

68   Convinced by their leaders that their way of life or their belief system is both superior to others and is allegedly 'supported by God', they can be easily persuaded that their fundamental values and way of life is under threat. Once this threat has been internalised and a powerful sense of fear generated, it is a small step to believing that violence is justified and that a war must be waged to preserve the way of life that has been pre-ordained for them. As several authors observe, secular ideas can also be held religiously – extreme nationalism, communism and fascism have functioned religiously insofar as adherents are passionate in their conviction and motivation and are prepared to die, but also to kill, for their beliefs.

69   This is particularly pertinent today as leaders use single identity categorisations of the world to garner support for wider missions that have to do with their own bid for political and economic power, nationally and internationally. Leaders for whom their own political positioning is a primary goal will inevitably play down the identities and interests that 'their' group shares with others. They well know that it is when people come together on the basis of identities outside constructed dualisms – when they meet and act as women, as young people, as citizens of a state or as people who share a regional identity, a political outlook or an artistic interest – that relationships based on mutual understanding develop, that violence is eschewed, and respect comes to characterise their interactions. Violence cannot be maintained between those who understand and respect each other. It can only be sustained with a breakdown of respect and understanding.

70   It is these multiple identities and this sort of connectedness that the Commonwealth represents and that it tries to support through its different activities. From the Commonwealth perspective, each nation is first and foremost a society of individuals that have multiple sources of affiliation and many bases of relating to each other.

71   The aim in future must be to strive even harder to recognise and nurture connections between groups on the basis of their multiple identities in order to avoid the pressure of being coalesced into polarised worlds. Efforts can be made at many levels. The starting point is personal awareness. Each of us can resist the tendency of identity politics to ignore the complexity and multiplicity of our identities through broadening our understanding of the richness of human identity. A Hutu who is roused to hostility

against a Tutsi can be reminded that they are both Rwandans, both Africans, perhaps even both Kigalians. He should be asked to recognise, too, that they share a human identity. Even though the British, French and Germans tore each other apart in 1914–1918, they now recognise each other, with little difficulty, as fellow Europeans.

Chapter 3: Poverty, Inequality and Humiliation

Poverty and inequality – links to violence

72　　There has been a great deal of debate about the linkages between disadvantage and discord. Various causal relationships have been suggested and explored in respect of a wide variety of conflicts. Some are more persuasive than others, but none, we believe, are compelling. The fundamental point is that, since even extreme poverty by itself does not necessarily lead to violence, where violence does occur other further factors must be in play.

73　　Poverty needs to be addressed in its own right and on the basis of commitments made by individual countries and the international community to achieve the Millennium Development Goals. But poverty alone does not automatically make people violent nor, in particular, does it lead to terrorism.

74　　To illustrate that poverty is rarely single-handedly responsible for group violence it is instructive to consider the connections between these phenomena in Northern Ireland, Britain and Kolkata (Calcutta), India. Successful efforts to reduce economic inequalities in Northern Ireland during the 1970s and 1980s did not greatly impact in the short term on the course of the Troubles. Although they helped to assuage some Catholic grievances on the economic and social fronts, these policies did little to address the essentially political grievances of the Catholic/Nationalists, which were about the very legitimacy of the state itself. At the same time they antagonised Loyalist/Protestants (some of whom were also disadvantaged) who felt themselves being surreptitiously betrayed by the British.

75　　In Britain, for example, opening up new economic opportunities in economically disadvantaged areas will not necessarily assuage feelings of alienation and grievance amongst black young people in inner urban areas who do not have access to good schools and employment-related networks. They are five times more likely to be stopped and searched by the police in London than are white young people.[x] Here, the actual problem is the perception of discrimination and disrespect in policing policy which cannot be overcome without a real partnership being established between the community and those who police the community.

76　　Kolkata is one of the poorest cities in India –in the world, even. However, it also has a very low crime rate – the lowest crime rate of any Indian city. This applies to the incidence of murder as well as to all other crimes. It also applies to crime against women, the incidence of which is very substantially lower than in any other Indian city.[xi]

---

x　　Stewart 2005: 7.

xi　　National Crime Records Bureau, Government of India 2006, 53 (table 1.8).

77   Crime is not an easy subject to explain with empirical generalisations, but there are some possible connections. One is that Kolkata has benefited from the fact that it has a long history of being a thoroughly mixed city where neighbourhoods have not been separated on ethnic or religious lines, as has occurred elsewhere. There are also other social influences, such as the huge role of shared cultural activities in the city, which mobilise the residents in co-operative directions.

78   The politics of the city may also play a part. The focus of left-leaning politics in Kolkata and West Bengal on deprivation related to class, and more recently gender, has made it harder to exploit religious differences to instigate riots against minorities, as has happened elsewhere – for example against Muslims and Sikhs in Mumbai and Ahmedabad. Cultural and social factors (and sometimes the absence of such factors), as well as features of political economy, are therefore important in understanding violence in the world today; they demand integrated attention as they are rarely separable.

79   More direct than the relationship between poverty and violence are the links between inequality, particularly economic inequality, and violence. There are a number of reasons why socio-economic marginalisation or disadvantage can be linked to patterns of violent conflict. These will normally relate to both subjectively perceived and objectively measured material inequalities, and a sense of injustice about those inequalities, as well as to a combination of other factors that are specific to the situation.

80   Objective as well as perceived disadvantage can interplay with one another. Thus, one group has, or is perceived to have, the land, the well-paid jobs, the best services, and the other has very limited access to these. In other words we need to assess the evenness or unevenness of the opportunity structures that exist and to take a long look at how far access and outcomes are, or can become, open to weaker groups. Patterns of disadvantage may be to do with discrimination (in jobs, housing), long-institutionalised cultural attitudes and structural inequalities (racism, the legacy of migration, lack of citizenship status), the apparent lack of government moves to put in place policies and laws to redress these inequalities, or other causes.

Rationales for intervention

81   What matters from the perspective of public policy is the degree to which inequality, particularly where it is deeply ingrained over time, can be tackled by extending opportunity structures.

82   In these circumstances the state should intervene to, in effect, represent and sponsor the interests of the powerless.

83 When socio-economic inequality is widely evident, acknowledged, and linked to opportunity structures, interventions can aim to correct economic distortions or deliver a fairer outcome. For example, the exclusion of a specific group from particular labour market opportunities may be experienced in daily terms as discrimination. Enlightened public policy can correct the current poor use of labour, which disadvantages both those who experience discrimination and the society as a whole, which is damaged by structural inequality and unfairness.

84 The public interest, crudely speaking, lies in bearing down on discriminatory and exclusionary practices in order to deliver benefits for the excluded or oppressed group (arguably helpful to the group) and all groups (compelling in the interests of all). The short-run loss of benefits for advantaged groups is something that must be managed in the meantime, perhaps through cushioning devices and open explanation and dialogue, if an adverse reaction is not to occur.

85 The first task in tackling inequality is to acknowledge that it exists. There must be a common, shared understanding of the problem.

Embedded inequality can be harder to tackle

86 Inequalities are more consequential when they are clearly perceived and linked with other divisions. Purely economic measures of inequality, such as the degree of disparity between the wealthiest and poorest groups in a society, are aggravated when minorities are disproportionately represented at the lower end of the economic scale. For example, when the people in the bottom groups in terms of income have different non-economic characteristics, in terms of race (such as being black rather than white), or immigration status (such as being recent arrivals rather than older residents), then the significance of the economic inequality is substantially magnified by its coupling with other divisions.

87 Unrest often reflects the strong effects of such coupling (for example, in the turmoil in the periphery of Paris, France and other cities in the autumn of 2005). The same degree of economic inequality may be much more explosive in one case than in another, when it occurs in combination with disparities in other social characteristics. In a global context, the proliferation of satellite television means that people in many poorer nations have a window into the lives of those in richer countries, and see the difference.

88 Violence, when it erupts, can seem mis-targeted when it is not directed at the obvious suspects (the government, large global corporations such as mining and oil companies), but instead at other groups in the area – those who are poor too but are seen to be benefiting in a local context and even if only marginally – from the presence of global

corporations. Battles for 'crumbs from the table' may also have historical roots – the unequal distribution today of mineral wealth reignites the memory of previous imbalances. Where people of particular sub-groups have greater access to these 'crumbs', this inequality must be diluted through opening up educational and vocational opportunities.

89   Perceptions of inequality can, paradoxically, also be felt by the relatively powerful, not just the relatively powerless. In this case the issue is generally a fear of losing control of a resource to which they have previously had access or about which they have a sense of entitlement.

90   This accounts for the antipathy of existing residents towards newly arrived migrants in the same economic class ('they are after our jobs'), to say nothing of existing settled migrants who face new competition for scarce resources. Not surprisingly, this antipathy is greater if the existing residents are poor themselves and have had to struggle to get a foothold in the job market. The last thing they want is to give up this tenuous position to people who will accept even lower wages. Their own loss is seen as directly caused by the gain of others.

91   Violence is therefore often occasioned by a fear of losing out on something. State violence also falls into this category. When the police or army are ordered to fire on crowds of demonstrators it is often because the government is already on the back foot. The violence is instrumental – it is used to suppress opposition but also to inspire fear, all in the name of regaining or maintaining political control.

92   Yet inequality, even severe inequality, does not inevitably lead to violence or, necessarily, even to protest. Huge inequalities exist between groups that live together without incident. This may be because the inequality has been internalised and the minority group feels its position is 'natural'. It may also be because they are aware of the inequality but do not make an issue of it – perhaps they are recent migrants and are prepared to put up with hardship because they hope for betterment in the future and for the sake of their children (which can store up problems which arise in the second and third generation of immigrant families).

93   Lack of protest may also be for pragmatic reasons; if protest has been tried before and met with a violent response then putting up with inequality may be a choice. Perhaps the growth of the economy and the prospect of educational advancement inspire hope. If the minority group can appeal to existing mechanisms for complaint and redress – if the political process allows for voice and the courts work well – inequality may be countenanced in the belief that their voice will be heard and their situation improved in the longer term. The Commission is keen to stress that objective material inequality does not mean people automatically protest, let alone choose violence.

Triggers for violence will vary

94   So what additional factors are normally present when violent conflict occurs? And how is violence sustained, given its enormously destructive impacts – for individuals, for communities, for nations? We have already alluded to one often missed element: the way in which various identities are truncated to one dimension which is then understood and presented as a fundamental clash of values, civilisations or belief systems.

95   In short, it is only with instigation that a grievance (for example over the unequal distribution of a resource) comes to be interpreted as an attack on the identity of a group. The message that must be conveyed and take root is: (a) 'This is happening because you are Kurds or Shias, Catholics or Protestants, Kosovars' – or whoever – and (b) 'There is no way of defending what is ours (and our self-respect) other than through violence'.

96   One of the legacies of colonialism is that it left in place populations already demarcated in terms of single identities and therefore potentially open to this sort of message. In many post-colonial countries racial, ethnic, and religious identities became politically and legally institutionalised through deliberate and planned processes of decolonisation and nation-building, resulting in clearly differentiated populations within bounded categories of identity, as well as simple distinctions of majority and minority.

97   In many of these countries, group privilege and rights were and continue to be officially entrenched in the institutions, processes, and practices of the nation-state, thereby reproducing multiple disparities among groups who have been classified and administered as distinct and unequal. In such circumstances group mobilisation can easily take place along the fault-lines of identity.

But humiliation can also have links to disrespect and violence

98   Feelings of humiliation can also be powerful contributors to a sense of disrespect and grievance. Humiliation is born from current or remembered ill-treatment, often over decades and even centuries, so that after some time people's energy and self-esteem ebbs away. Their sense of what is right is no longer taken into account and they are left with a sense of acute injustice. Violence that is underlain by feelings of humiliation and shaming can be experienced as a form of retaliation, a fighting back for self-esteem and a statement of self-worth.

99   There are many examples of how humiliation has been imposed on peoples and communities and on how it has (though not always) lead to retaliatory action.

100   The Independent Commission on Africa led by Albert Tevoedjre argued in their 2003 report that Africa is a 'continent of humiliation'. They considered the factors that have

made for its subjugation and denigration over the last millennium. These include the transatlantic slave trade, the colonisation process and the fragmentation of the continent before and during the colonial period, the systematic devaluation of Africa's natural and human resources through an unjust exchange system and the portrayal of Africa as a continent of poverty in the media. While addressing underlying causes is essential, the Tevoedire Report also sees winning the 'war against humiliation' as the primary task for Africa in this millennium, through institution- and capacity-building and empowerment.[xii]

101   The narrative of humiliation that is articulated and received in many Muslim societies is an important theme amongst commentators analysing the root causes of growing Islamist fervour. Some have gone further and sought to explain today's tensions in terms of a sense of collective humiliation felt by declining Islamic empires from the sixteenth century onwards. Even the most casual observer acknowledges the contemporary dynamics of global Islam in which the sense of the honour or dignity of Muslims is under attack. A perception of humiliation at the hands of western, secularly-minded governments and publics is a core element of the narrative.

102   In a similar vein the Palestinian readiness to be recruited for violent 'retaliation' against Israel is made possible by the sense of humiliation which has been caused by displacement, and a sense of oppression and statelessness.

103   Migrant populations, those that have moved from their place of origin either through their own volition, through forceful removal or through their vulnerability to poverty and unequal treatment may also feel a sense of individual or group humiliation. This can occur however short the journey. Migrants who are not afforded the rights of citizens and who have an identity as 'non-persons', who feel their energy and enthusiasm and skills are consistently ignored when they try to find work or housing, or who are forced through trafficking into degrading work like prostitution, are likely to feel humiliated as a group but also at a personal level. Such humiliation may never manifest itself in a public way – there may be little chance to do this without reprisal. In other situations humiliation can fuel feelings of grievance at a very basic level and, if other circumstances are present, result in violent retaliation in subsequent generations.

104   Like poverty and inequality, feelings of humiliation can be eased and sometimes even healed over time. None of these things is immutable. One of the ways this has historically happened in the case of humiliation is through programmes of 'reconciliation' and inclusion after prolonged periods of conflict. This is discussed below in the context of breaking down historical narratives of grievance and rebuilding relationships on a different footing.

---

xii   Tevoedjre, 2002.

Chapter 4: History, Grievance and Conflict

History and grievance are often intertwined

105   Remembered injustices, including those that occurred decades, even centuries before, play an important role in justifying and sustaining many conflicts. Certain remembered processes, the most obvious being colonialism, slavery and the Holocaust, leave a backlog of potentially flammable grievances. Feelings of grievance around a sense of historical injustice need to be understood, not in the sense of what actually happened (this is always open to interpretation) but in terms of what they mean today. However long ago events occurred, it is their interpretation in the light of current circumstances that gives them relevance. These form a backdrop against which more immediate grievances become significant.

106   There are various examples of historic, retained grievance that shape the way in which potential conflict can be kept alive. The Commission observed that the nineteenth-century Irish Famine not only represented massive deprivation and hardship, but also led to deep-seated feelings of anger and disrespect that continue to live on in the minds of later generations that cannot have been directly affected (and sometimes more strongly in the diaspora than in those left behind).

107   In the context of peace and power-sharing in Northern Ireland today, wise and perceptive policy has been aided by an appreciation of, and sensitivity towards, persisting, subliminal grievances on all sides of the traditional fault-line of faith. The recollection of a past event as divisive as the Battle of the Boyne has been remembered in a way that, since the division of the island, has 'justified' enmity between the two sides.

108   Current leaders have been alive to the need not only to build new political structures but also to address and combat this kind of justification. Failure to do so, they have concluded, would result in a peace that was, and could only ever be, skin deep. What was required, by contrast, is something more ambitious that recognises the layered and uncritical way in which past grievance has been left to fester and potentially fuel enmity today.

Narratives of grievance can be pervasive

109   How the story of grievance is told to one's own children, community and to others, how it is then reproduced in the media and often, eventually, in school textbooks (thereby institutionalising it for generations of young people) is an important element in the maintenance and even escalation of disputes, including violent ones.

110   Such narratives bind a community together and unite them around a common cause and this can be positive. But it can also result in portraying the 'other' in a wholly negative light, divesting them of any moral authority or legitimacy; make feelings of hate and

distrust 'normal'; and, in extreme cases, be used to justify violence. That is why it is important to nurture across all groups within society a sense of shared common destiny that can transcend long-felt grievances and humiliations.

111   It has been the particular narratives created around shared Muslim global grievance that have been among the most powerful in recent years. Muslims continue to suffer, these narratives will say, simply because the world does not care, or because powerful non-Muslims, especially in the West, feel hatred of Muslims or contempt for Islam. This is a powerful narrative with considerable potential to mobilise opinion in a wide range of similar and dissimilar countries. It is also a narrative that can and has been underscored by attachment to the Muslim *Ummah* or sense of religious community and common purpose.

112   Sometimes narratives of grievance continue even after peace breaks out. In some cases, it may be that grassroots combatants feel undermined by the peace agreements made in their name – this was the reaction of some loyalist paramilitary groups in Northern Ireland to the Good Friday Agreement. Those involved in gangs or paramilitary groups may also have personal reasons for continuing to fight – it may afford them status amongst their peers or they may be making a living from the violence. Others may always have been involved in violence, since childhood, and never have had the opportunity to stand back and re-think the history of the conflict from their own perspective, but also from the perspectives of others.

113   Importantly, and as we have noted, in order to understand and respect others it is first necessary to be understood and respected oneself.

Reconciliation, often led by women, is a key to healing

114   When conflict ends and reconciliation begins, history needs to be revisited and reinterpreted so that people can move on. Ties that joined the two communities in the past need to be re-emphasised so that scant memories about what times used to be like can be re-ignited. If there was no previous contact, then the affinities they currently share (loyalty to a region, aspects of culture or language) need to be emphasised. Both women and civil society groups have played enormously important roles in reconciliation and peace-building and it is worth considering why their contributions are so significant.

115   Whether women were involved as combatants or not, they are likely to share aspects of their identity and their experience of warfare with women on the 'other' side. Like men, women know what it means to have sons, brothers, husbands and even mothers and daughters, who fought and died in conflict; like men, they know what it means to be displaced. But they are more likely to suffer high rates of maternal and child mortality and low rates of access to education and health care and to experience

exclusion from public life, and they will more often know what it is not to be recognised as full citizens. Women who have survived wars must find ways to live with the gross injustices that have filled their past and are haunting their present – acts of discrimination and violence committed before, during and even after conflict.

116   It is their common experience as women that makes women's role in peace-building so critical, a role that is now formally recognised in UN Security Council Resolution 1325. This resolution attempts to develop a more systematic way of consulting with and involving women in peace and reconstruction processes. The Commission recognises this crucial role of women, in the hope that their experiences, priorities and solutions contribute more than they have before towards the reconstruction of societies based on inclusive governance. Women can bring some particular strengths and perspectives. For example the fruits of their experience in relating through networks of relationships rather than hierarchical structures is especially important given what we have said earlier about the role of networking in 'government through respectful dialogue'.

117   In Rwanda for example, Tutsi and Hutu widows first came together to take care of war orphans, and are now supporting them by selling their woven baskets in the global market. Women ex-combatants, with first-hand experience as both perpetrators and victims of violence, met to share their experiences and learn ways to manage trauma, and a few have become trainers in the Demobilization and Reintegration Commission, ensuring attention to women's needs in disarmament, demobilisation and reintegration. Most notably, by ensuring the inclusion of a 30 per cent quota for women in parliament in the new Constitution, Rwandan women ultimately won a full 49 per cent share – the highest in the world.[xiii] In Burundi, women from each of the 19 parties to the Arusha peace negotiations came together in the All Party Burundi Women's Peace Conference in July 2000 to formulate an agenda for peace and reconstruction that would guarantee women's rights to rebuild their society alongside men, thereby positioning themselves to enter the political process.[xiv] And through the International Women's Commission for a Just and Sustainable Palestinian–Israeli Peace, prominent Palestinian and Israeli women have come together to advance the peace process and speak with one voice to global leaders.

118   It is instructive to look at how India has opened up the panchayat system, enabling women to take on leadership positions at the local level. Many of these women, nearly 1 million, have been trained in how to analyse local budgets from a gender perspective, making the link between national gender equality policies and actual spending to implement these policies. By looking at budget expenditures, community members are able to ensure that a greater percentage of local resources are spent to provide clean water, health clinics or better local transport systems. They have also engaged in social

xiii   UNIFEM 2004-05 and UNIFEM 2006-07.

xiv   UNIFEM 2000.

audits, demanding public review of income and expenditure of village councils and holding officials accountable for addressing, or failing to address, local needs. The positive results of these initiatives show the importance of building women's agency from the bottom up.

119   The role of civil society in post-conflict situations is important for the same reason: civil society groups and organisations can bring together people on the basis of identities they share, not those that have previously divided them. When people meet, for example, as journalists, business people, educationalists or trade union members, and when they are drawn from both sides of previous divisions, they not only bring with them a ready-made network of contacts but also a means of communicating with those contacts. They then have within their grasp the possibility of generating new, jointly developed messages about new ways of relating to each other and working together.

120   The rehabilitation of young people in the immediate aftermath of severe conflict is one of the most challenging tasks facing civil society organisations. We are just beginning to understand the profoundly damaging effects on the personalities of young people who grow up in conflict-ridden societies. Often in the aftermath they find it difficult to live in a peaceful society and have stable personal relationships, and the rate of youth suicides may increase significantly. Where child soldiers have been part of the landscape of violent conflict, this task can appear daunting given the way in which violence has been habitually embedded in young, formative minds. One programme that has worked in Liberia promotes amputees who have lost limbs in the conflict to take up competitive soccer. People who had been on opposite sides of the fourteen-year conflict in Liberia now play soccer together, often in the same team. The team members themselves see playing soccer together as a great expression of reconciliation.

121   Another important group of people in post-conflict situations are those previously involved in the fighting, including those who have themselves committed atrocities. Very few ex-combatants are given the chance to be listened to and to put their point of view to the wider world. And yet this was a major achievement of South Africa's Peace and Reconciliation Commission, an approach that has since been emulated in many other countries (and had also been used earlier in a number of other countries, particularly in Latin America).

122   The Truth and Reconciliation Commission (TRC) was established in South Africa in 1995 in order to start healing some of the deep wounds of the Apartheid years. The main vehicle of the TRC for this purpose was public storytelling, the aim being to establish a picture of the causes, nature and extent of the violations that had occurred during the Apartheid period. This included both the perspectives of the victims and the motives and perspectives of those responsible for the violations. Amnesty was granted to everyone who fully disclosed what had gone on and this apparently helped enormously in restoring the human dignity of the victims.

123   The TRC thus allowed individuals to tell their story from their own point of view, and to be heard. This proved a major step in the reconciliation process. But it is important to emphasise that its success depended in large part on the fact that it was not – and did not seek to be – a process of redress, and that it was constructed in a particular historic and socio-cultural context.[xv] While the exact process cannot simply be repeated in precisely the same way elsewhere, there are important general lessons here on the use of constructive interaction that is an integral part of the civil route to peace.

xv   Mani 2002.

Chapter 5: Political Participation

Dialogue and inclusion

124   In the previous four chapters, this report outlined some of the reasons why respect and understanding are so important at the present time, and the relevance of the Commonwealth approach in engendering a sense of these basic values. It also discussed some of the conceptual issues that underlie violence and concluded that a deeper analysis of these should first inform public debate, and only then feed in to the development of new policies or actions.

125   This chapter begins with an analysis of the constraints that all countries face in ensuring the whole of their population – not just elites and holders of public office – feel fully involved in what has been termed 'government by discussion'. This is about more than putting the right political processes in place, it is also about how these processes are facilitated so that they are truly inclusive – it is the 'how' of political behaviour, not just the 'what'.

126   Furthermore, ways of engendering a sense of belonging, particularly for groups that are traditionally excluded from politics, are discussed. The chapter also considers how political participation might be broadened and extended in situations of peace as well as in post-conflict situations. Going beyond this analysis, therefore, the chapter begins to look at public policy and the messages for governments and civil society. This dual focus – on both substantive analysis and policy messages – is also reflected in future chapters.

An emphasis on the 'how' of political participation

127   A sense of exclusion can arise even in well-established, participatory democratic systems. This is because political inclusion is not only about the form that political systems take (for example, the type of electoral system), but, just as importantly, about how political participation is facilitated throughout the political cycle (and not just at elections). Thus, how debate is managed in local and national political forums, including parliament itself, will reflect on the extent to which the rules of engagement, written or unwritten, provide a containing environment for expression of conflict. It will also be reflected in a context that does, or does not, also allow members to express their strong concerns and feel that they have been listened to – and thus accorded respect.

128   Different perceptions co-exist about the role of opposition parties. Whilst some act primarily as though they are the party in waiting, and therefore spend time consolidating their power base, others focus on the real job of opposition. This is to hold the government of the day to account by listening to the experience of their constituents and being sufficiently well-informed by evidence and argument to support or question the impact of current or planned public policies. Again, the latter approach will make

people feel represented and included; the former, typically, will not. The representative duties of parliamentarians are obviously of great importance for the functioning of a civil approach to peace and the avoidance of extremism.

129   Apart from the workings of parliaments, other aspects of democratic systems are also important if 'government by discussion' is to have real meaning. For example, it is critical that people who purport to represent different factions, including parties in conflict, really are representative in a meaningful way, and have representative views that can be attributed to their supporters. All too often, debate can be taken over, or misappropriated, by vocal and more extreme members of a group. These people may not have the actual standing or authority they claim to have; yet their tendency to grab the headlines with inflammatory remarks tends to be seized upon by the media. The perceptions of the general community are then skewed into believing that all members of the group agree with these inflammatory and disturbing statements.

130   Seeking out those who do in fact represent the group, and do so in a balanced and good-tempered way, is essential and it is a delicate task for government and civil society. The calmer, yet more authentic, leaders and would-be leaders within communities may be repelled by polemic and aggressive behaviour and language. They may, therefore, quite rationally opt not to participate because of the tone, the nature of the discussion, and the manner with which their case is (supposedly) being put. Extremists may also be more likely to be heard if the government does not adequately heed parliament and other legitimate or reasonable representatives.

Communication and consultation styles matter

131   Styles of communication and consultation are particularly important for the participation of women and young people. If serious, experienced and well-intentioned people, with a strong sense of the common good, leave the discussion or never join it, this creates an opportunity for others who may have narrower self-seeking interests to step into the void.

132   In many countries, women are given limited opportunities to develop their skills in participative debate and decision-making at local or national level. In such circumstances, they cannot and do not contribute as equal partners to debates on the development of their communities or countries. One constraint is the absence of laws on gender equality broadly based on international human rights standards. However, the norms of patriarchy and generations of past practice also determine the extent of women's participation in politics at all levels.

133   Nevertheless, it is important to underline that there has been accelerating change in many parts of the Commonwealth on women's participation at the highest levels. The development over many years of a strong female presence in the legal system, in general, and the judiciary, in particular, has led to the appointment this year of the first

woman Chief Justice in Ghana, Justice Georgina Woode. These examples of public commitment to make constructive use of women's agency going well beyond the concern with women's well-being reflect the development over many years, under many governments, of a continuing concern to make an increasingly equal place for women in the legal profession. This is a development that increases the sense among all women that the law need not be blind to women's concerns, but in addition allows the gains from women's active agency to be utilised in the legal systems of these countries. The leadership, for example, of Judge Kate O'Regan on human rights legislation in the South African constitutional court, has greatly assisted the reach of the legal system in this newly democratic country.

134 Elsewhere, in Afghanistan, women participated in the Constitutional *Loya Jirga*[xvi] (Grand Assembly) elections in June 2002 and in drafting the new Constitution in 2004, and they stood as candidates in the parliamentary and provincial elections of 2005. With help from UN agencies (UNIFEM[xvii] and UNDP[xviii]), the women's participation project has also resulted in the adoption of a Constitution with strong provisions for gender equality, including a 25 per cent quota for women in the national and provincial assemblies (which has been achieved), and the formation of a women's caucus in parliament. Although the rise of insurgency, especially in rural areas, threatens these gains, a great deal has been achieved in women's participation in politics since the fall of the Taliban in 2001.

135 And, to offer one final example, Commonwealth countries in South Asia have a lesson to teach others – that is: that women can reach the pinnacle of power. In Sri Lanka, Sirimavo Bandaranaike became Prime Minister in1959. Her religious background was Buddhism. Indira Gandhi was elected more than once as the Head of the Indian Government. Benazir Bhutto became the first woman Prime Minister of her country, Pakistan, as the Muslim world's first female Head of Government. Bangladesh has produced more than one female political leader in Begum Khaleda Zia and Sheikh Hasina.

Young people's involvement requires nurturing

136 Many countries have mechanisms for consulting young people on political issues – for example, via dedicated surveys and more qualitatively by contacting young people's organisations and/or using research teams or interviewers to organise young people into focus groups in order to ascertain their views on a particular subject.

---

xvi   Loya Jirgas (Grand Assemblies) are called in Afghanistan irregularly, often by the ruler. They are attended by tribal/regional leaders, political, military and religious figures, royalty, government officials, etc. The meeting has no time limit, it continues until decisions are reached by consensus on the matter at hand.

xvii   United Nations Development Fund for Women.

xviii   United Nations Development Programme.

137   But very often this only goes so far; older, more established voices then take over to decide the public policy implications. This is particularly the case in contexts where relations of patriarchy and deference are strong. Young people do need positive role models in authority. But, crucially, they also need spaces in which to build their own confidence and capabilities and have their views taken into account.

138   Authority needs to be exercised in a way that does not end up marginalising the young and others with little formal voice.

139   Young people therefore emerge as an entry-point for political participation but also as an interest group and a vital resource. They have much more of a sense of the way the world is developing than the current generation of elders. We not only need young people in our families to show us how to work our new machines, we need them to help us design and work our new machinery of governance, and they need the opportunity to work together with groups of older people, as well as independently, to identify innovative ways of tackling deep-seated misconceptions and prejudices, first within their own age group, and then beyond it. There is something of an inter-generational division of labour to aim for:

> 'We need younger Community leaders to be enthusiastic and give a lead in drawing our communities together. Older people can suggest ways and means by which this can be achieved – but it is the up-and-coming generation of political, civil and religious leaders who need to take up the cause of mutual respect and understanding. For this, they will need training, but above all, enthusiasm, dedication and motivation'.[xix]

And civil society has an active role to play

140   In our striving for more liberal democratic societies we have perhaps focused too much on the sporadic involvement given by elections as the solution to the problem of involvement. A society based on 'government by discussion' requires a strong civil society that plays an active role in political debate. Civil society is, of course, very diverse and civil society groups have a range of functions, not all of which are aimed at increasing political voice.

141   Nonetheless research has shown that the 'empowered' citizen emerges gradually, often through local-level debates around jobs, housing or other tangible issues, and only later (sometimes a generation later) gains the independence and knowledge to engage with higher level state processes. Civil society organisations, even if they are not overtly political, can therefore provide the building blocks with which their members may engage with political processes in future, should they wish to.

xix   Gregorios 2007.

142   One striking example of this is the role that grassroots organisations played in combating the spread of HIV/AIDs in Australia in the early 1980s. It was at this time that Australia experienced a rapid increase in the incidence of HIV. Peaking in 1984, incidence rates then began to fall dramatically until around 1988.

143   For a long time, the success of early containment had been credited to national initiatives. Recent analysis,[xx] however, has shown that these initiatives – the establishment of research institutions, the provision of HIV testing and anti-retroviral drugs, all supported by significant government funding – all came *after* the decline in incidence rates had begun.

144   Well-organised grassroots activities and structures, by comparison, were in place by 1985. AIDS Action Committees (AACs) were created in major state capitals, the first as early as 1983. The first community-based organisation to create a dedicated office in the non-governmental AIDS sector was in place by 1984. And during this time, the medical profession began to rely on the Gay Health Update produced by the Victorian AIDS Council for information on how the epidemic was developing. Early reports in the press, the provision of clinical services and community activism all played a key role in Australia's success in combating the spread of HIV/AIDS.

145   Without government initiatives, the decline may not have lasted. This much is clear. But what the research does point to is the ability of community-based and non-governmental organisations to be pro-active; to successfully mobilise communities to provide early intervention and prevention. Governments should seek out organisations with this ability, and help them to build their capacity in a spirit of partnership.

Engendering a sense of belonging

146   For any society to create a common vision for itself, it is necessary for it to find effective ways to nurture a sense of belonging among all its members, including young people. These members are not merely required to be of that society, they are also entitled to be treated in a way that values them as integral to the society. They need to have a sense of being part of a common destiny and a shared future. For this reason alone, there has to be some public endorsement and acceptance of identity even if there are plural identities involved. As mentioned previously, it is preferable for richly textured and multi-layered identities not to be collapsed simplistically into identification based on a single characteristic only, be that racial, linguistic or religious.

147   A traditional liberal and democratic understanding of societal membership has in the past tended to focus on recognition of individuals as citizens. The concept of citizenship is indifferent to group identity or identities – the idea of citizenship does not

xx   Plummer and Irwin 2006.

differentiate or discriminate between people with different identities, it looks at national belonging alone. Identity based on citizenship can amount to an essential lubricant of common belonging and inclusion to work. The idea of national citizenship may be more important for certain groups than others, and may matter in differing ways from one group or context to another.

148   Faith-based organisations have a potentially crucial role and can do much to overcome the constraints that those in the political system may experience. In particular, faith bodies that develop strong bonding relationships among their own members can be in a better position to encourage bridging relationships with those of other faith-identity communities. This can lead to a stronger articulation by faith communities in general of faith and spiritual-oriented approaches to tackling social problems. The role of spirituality in better understanding and responding to the causes of religious extremism and violence is a potentially rich terrain that requires space for consideration.[xxi]

149   The task is to build the foundations of a community that is both cohesive as well as diverse in its composition. This involves several elements whereby:[xxii]

- There is a common vision and all communities have a sense of belonging.

- The diversity of people's different backgrounds and circumstances is appreciated and positively valued.

- Those from different backgrounds have similar opportunities. Language fluency and language barriers to entry into particular occupational categories are a prime example that can prevent this.

- Those from different backgrounds develop strong, positive relationships in the workplace, in schools and within neighbourhoods.

Confidence-building in conflict situations carries additional risks

150   Some very specific issues exist around dialogue in conflict situations, particularly when there has been outside military intervention. Even if military intervention is sanctioned by the United Nations, it does not mean that a UN force will be automatically welcomed or their presence accepted by local populations. Whether this happens will depend in large part on how the intervention is managed and how processes for dialogue with local leaders and people are developed. This involves literally how the actions of those on the ground are able to gain, or do not gain, the confidence of people and institutions. However bad the situation that led to the intervention, no occupying force can expect local support unless people themselves feel included and respected.

xxi   Taylor 2007.

xxii   Malik 2005.

Commonwealth principles in action

151   The Commonwealth is sometimes criticised for talking first, often, and for a very long time on an issue of contention without reaching any resolution. But this *Report of the Commission* endorses this approach as an essential way of dealing with problems of respect and understanding – as well as a way to reduce violence and the incidence and impact of terrorism.

152   Criticism of the Commonwealth approach fails to acknowledge that:

- The practical application of Commonwealth principles has yielded significant change in some of the largest conflicts of the contemporary world, such as South Africa.

- Practitioners of these principles have gained currency for their style of engagement that respects differences of identity and viewpoint.

- These principles place leaders in a strong and credible position in searching for the underlying causes of conflict and violence.

- The Commonwealth approach has fresh relevance as the reputation of more confrontationist approaches has begun to falter.

153   Talking alone cannot solve all the world's problems. It is doubtful what could have been achieved by talking for longer in Afghanistan, Yugoslavia or Rwanda as the events that occurred in all these places were not obviously due to a lack of dialogue but for other reasons. Sometimes conflict can escalate to extreme levels of violence so quickly (as in Rwanda) that face-to-face discussion is hard to achieve. But problems in Northern Ireland were resolved by talking, India and Pakistan are talking rather than going to war, and it is not beyond the bounds of possibility to believe that in the end relations between Israel and Palestine may yet be resolved through a long-term process of dialogue and deeper mutual respect and understanding.

Promoting democracy through institutional best practice

154   The Commonwealth is currently engaged in a wide range of activities designed to ensure adherence to best practice in democratic political participation. One example is the role of election observers – widely accepted as a mean to ensure that the processes of elections are fair and unbiased. This kind of intervention is especially valuable where recent past experience has meant that there is little public confidence in the democratic electoral process itself.

155   Election observation is an example of confidence building in that it is designed to deter the use of domineering or oppressive behaviour by particular groups, through independent documentation of the election process by third parties. Independence lies at its heart, indeed, the Commonwealth 'brand' is widely trusted perhaps more than any

other. The Commonwealth offers election observation only when invited and so all parties have an incentive to comply with international standards and a reason to accept the observers' judgments.

156   There is a rub, however, namely that election observation is an intervention that comes late in the process and inevitably avoids looking at behaviour and standards beforehand. A more holistic picture reveals that intimidation, exclusion and other indirect threats to general public confidence may be present a long time before an election is staged. The problem, therefore, largely occurs further upstream and needs to be tackled at that earlier point.

157   Limiting these influences may be laudable during an election process, but the problems may have set in well before the election campaign begins. There can be longstanding negative attitudes, practices and behaviour which become more plainly expressed during an election process. There is, therefore, a strong case to look at:

- how interventions to promote democratic engagement might be used in the period between election campaigns; and

- how to grow the capacity of local institutions and groups as buttresses for democracy.

158   The latter include genuinely independent electoral commissions to oversee behaviour and adherence to fair processes including funding arrangements for parties and candidates, parliamentary secretariats to support the scrutiny functions of parliamentarians, and finally technical assistance to election observer missions that train and support good practice among local election officials.

159   A bigger challenge even than this lies in finding new ways to promote legitimate and credible interaction between governments and oppositions after the elections in different Commonwealth countries. In circumstances where electoral systems are based on a single majority-simple plurality (SMSP) principle, the outcome can often be a winner-takes-all situation triggered by being the first-past-the-post. Holding a monopoly of executive power carries with it serious consequences and risks. Chief among these is the on-going need to involve and retain the confidence of opposition parties and candidates who do not participate in government.

160   Opposition involvement and buy-in to the process is valuable yet often elusive. Specifically, their involvement is critical to sustain backing for the legitimacy of the political system as opposed to the government of the day. In other words, the task is to strike a balance: to nurture backing for the office of government whilst remaining agnostic towards the office-holder.

161   Executive dominance of this kind is a direct cause for concern in itself. But it is particularly dangerous if it is in the hands of a particular ethnic or religious group,

perhaps via a party system that is built around ethno-religious lines. Interventions to help broaden out 'government by discussion' in systems where power is concentrated in the hands of the executive can be pursued in various ways. For leaders, such broadening can happen in three main ways, (these strategies are not mutually exclusive but each involves a particular area of concentration). They can:

- try to dilute the executive monopoly of power by building in some element of power sharing;

- strengthen the balancing role of parliament and the judiciary; and

- support media, civil society and community-based efforts to demand greater accountability.

162   Building in an element of power sharing to the executive has been addressed, for instance by establishing extra-parliamentary forums in which government–opposition interaction is routinised, and where complex issues to do with public confidence in the democratic process are aired. The Commonwealth's Good Offices work has sought to further this kind of assistance. The Commonwealth Ministerial Action Group acts as a guardian of the fundamental principles of the Commonwealth. It is also possible for Commonwealth countries to turn to other Commonwealth states for expert assistance and advice, as the UK did from time to time in the Northern Ireland process.

Chapter 6: The Role of the Media and Communication

Media messages convey important influences

163 Mass media and other forms of communication technology have an enormous influence in helping to shape public opinion and underlying sentiment. Newspapers, TV and radio are all important sources of basic information about other people and other places and this can itself help to engender understanding if presented in a fair, even-handed and non-inflammatory way.

164 The media is also an important accountability mechanism: it raises important issues, corruption for example, that might otherwise never be publicly debated or addressed. The media also has an important role in stimulating governments to take action on social policy: although stories about migrants or refugees might reinforce prejudice in some quarters, they also expose problems that need to be addressed, for example poor living conditions or lack of access to services, the citizenship status of migrants, the response of local communities to their settlement and so on.

165 But the media can also, in some cases, become an instrument for the dissemination of false and inflammatory messages and values that do not promote respect or well-tempered dialogue and discussion. Negative messages can divide communities and can help perpetuate the stereotypes that nurture violence.

166 Media portrayals can sometimes serve to exacerbate the narrative of oppositional forces and irreconcilable, value-based differences. The media often prefers to dwell on conflict, since conflict and drama sell newspapers and attract an audience. This inevitably means that the more extreme points of view get airtime rather than the feelings of the majority of citizens that may have more accommodating and balanced perspectives. For example, during the 1994 Rwandan genocide, the state-supported Radio Télévision Libre des Mille Collines (RTLM) station broadcast hate propaganda against Tutsis, moderate Hutus, Belgians and the United Nations, and was used as a tool to organise massacres. And even when the media are truly independent, there can be a tendency by some (though not all) of the media to oversimplify the complexity of current problems and reduce the news to catch phrases and sound bytes – on the assumption that people want drama and entertainment rather than informed analysis. An emphasis on the constructive role of the media, which we strongly support, has to go with a realistic recognition of the problems that the media have reason to guard against.

And new media serve to shape outlooks more directly

167 The internet has radically changed the way in which people communicate and connect with each other. As a means of social interaction, the web brings people together –

friends, family, young people, or complete strangers that share interests or objectives – and this can foster a sense of belonging and identity. The web, however, has also been used to target people, mainly young users, to radicalise them into specific belief systems and divisive ways of seeing the world.

168   Some constructive means of linking like-minded peaceful groups across dispersed regions already exists – including those such as 'Youth for a Sustainable Future', an email discussion group founded by young people in the Pacific to discuss issues affecting themselves and the region.

169   However, the riots in Cronulla, in southern Sydney, Australia, in December 2005 are an interesting illustration of the role of the media and modern forms of communication like text messaging in a less peaceful direction. For some time, there had been a growing escalation of hostilities between some members of the local Anglo-Australian community and Middle Eastern people at Cronulla Beach. Over a 36-hour period there was a rapid build-up of violence, and a reaction 24 hours later by those who had been subjected to violence, to a great extent using organised text messaging.

170   Cronulla beach became the contested space between people of Middle Eastern background on the one hand and the 'traditional' Anglo-Australians for whom Cronulla was the home of their traditional surf beach culture. In the weeks leading up to the conflict, the media reported stories of beachgoers who complained that they had had sand flicked in their faces by young men of Middle Eastern background while they were playing soccer, and there were other reports of Middle Eastern men who made offensive remarks about women who were wearing bikinis and other clothes that the men considered immodest and offensive. The conflict escalated one Saturday afternoon in early December 2005, stoked by a huge proliferation by white youths of text messaging up and down the coastal beaches of Sydney.

171   On a more positive note, the riots caused a great deal of reflection about the nature and impact of some media coverage, and soul searching about how to mitigate a sense of exclusion and hostility by some groups. Surf lifesaving clubs, the bastion of surf and local community culture, have been opened up to members of different groups. There has been a successful programme to encourage young Muslim people to train as lifesavers, and modesty-driven adaptations to traditional women's swimming costumes have been designed for young Muslim women who want to enjoy the beach and participate in community activities.

172   Sometimes the internet has been used for fomenting group violence. Taking the rough with the smooth, an awareness of this problem is important, while building on the constructive role of the media and public dialogue.

The media can have innovative roles in breaking down conflict

173   Other media initiatives have been successful at increasing the inclusion of previously marginalised groups by providing them with a means of expressing their views. Positive results have also resulted from the creation of channels through which older, familiar binary disputes can be broken down and re-imagined in ways that highlight common interests that transcend warring boundaries.

174   In the occupied Palestinian territory, an on-going Palestinian initiative aims to promote gender equity through media capacity-building and outreach. The programme created networks of local media professionals (male and female) in the different communities, trained them to produce, print and broadcast programmes on women's lives and issues, and fostered relationships, collaboration and information-sharing between women leaders and media professionals. Training was provided to women leaders in media presentation skills, and to public information officers in media advocacy campaigns. As a result, several long-term relationships were established between women's organisations and television and radio stations, enabling women to continue sharing information and informing broadcasts. This initiative for the Promotion of Global Dialogue and Democracy (MIFTAH) is supported by UNIFEM.

175   Another interesting example of a direct effort to promote goodwill between nations was the US government's sponsorship of the band *Audioslave* on a tour of Cuba. In what seemed to be a sort of peace offering, few were able to discern exactly what the US government was trying to achieve, or what the Cuban government was receiving in return. The spectacle of *Audioslave* trying to 'make friends' with Cuba with the endorsement of the US government, in a way that US foreign policy had failed to achieve over almost half a century, is a powerful reminder of the influence of music.

176   The world of journalism has also grasped opportunities to promote understanding in conflict situations. In Northern Ireland, just before the Good Friday Agreement, the editors of a Catholic nationalist newspaper and a Protestant unionist newspaper developed a joint initiative. They asked their readers to 'Call this number if you say "Yes to Peace"'. The fact that the two main newspapers on opposite sides of the divide ran the same text with the same notice was very powerful. A total of 145,000 calls were made, and with a local population of only 1.5 million people, this amounted to a significant one-in-ten response rate.

177   This initial success led to another interesting venture where each editor wrote an editorial in favour of peace for the same day, and sent it to each other in advance, working on the drafts until they had a single editorial to which they could both sign up. As a result, Protestants and Catholics in Northern Ireland could read the same words in 'their' separate newspapers, and know that the editors they trusted had been able to express the same sentiments, while remaining true to their interests. It was a powerful piece of innovative journalism and became something of a story in itself.

178   A broader task, jointly faced by Commonwealth members and media professionals, is to develop a more critical understanding of international issues. The *UN Alliance of Civilisations* report highlighted this area for special concern, and noted that taking corrective measures would greatly help to inform publics in various countries in a balanced way about international issues. Professional schools of journalism and media are particularly important in achieving this kind of wider orientation of the role of journalists and other media professionals. Media responsibility is the ethical correlative of media freedom.

Chapter 7: Young People and Education

Young people and the respect and understanding agenda

179   More than 60 per cent of the Commonwealth's population are aged under 30 years; the proportion is closer to three-quarters in some member countries. Young people are the inheritors of a changing world – its economic distributions, social positions, cultural identities and historical narratives. They need not be passive recipients of these things; with appropriate support and political will young people can be an active, positive force for development, locally, nationally and internationally.

180   But for this to happen, they need to be seen and treated as potential assets and engaged in processes of dialogue and decision-making. They need to be included in forums where it is possible to listen and participate, but also to put forward their own point of view and have their own narratives heard, discussed and debated. There also needs to be a deeper understanding of the inter-generational transmission of narratives.

181   In this regard, we have to recognise the critical importance of school principals and administrators – and eventually teachers – as leaders who can potentially change social reality by the way in which they manage their schools. Schools, after all, often have diverse workforces themselves (that is, teachers) and the principal can set the tone for the entire school and thereby influence the way in which the children grow up thinking about issues such as community, religion and violence.

182   Most young people enter workforces that have either a limited demand for their skills or where there are very few opportunities for decent work at all. Between 2000 and 2015 an estimated 1 billion young men and women will enter the labour market and try to find work – but there will not be 1 billion jobs waiting for them. In terms of both the uncertainty of employment and the fact that as young people they are simply not accorded respect in many societies, they are in some senses a marginalised group. But they are also unlikely to self-identity *as* a group, still less to organise as a social force.

183   The Commission notes that it is essential to think about respect and understanding in an inter-generational context, and to be acutely aware of the impact of societal norms, particularly patriarchy and deference, on the self-confidence and development of young people. In many situations, authority structures need to be reconstructed so they do not silence young people, and particularly young women and other groups whose voice is normally stilled through a reference to 'tradition' or 'custom'.

184   When young people are disenfranchised or humiliated or made to feel that they have little say and no future, they may become drawn into movements or ideologies that appear to guarantee them a place in the world and give them a solid identity. In some instances, inspiring or forceful leaders may draw them into conflicts as combatants,

literally as foot soldiers. World-wide an estimated 300,000 people under the age of 18 are now, or have recently been, involved in armed conflict, and another 500,000 have been recruited into military or paramilitary forces.

185 But young people need not be only the victims or perpetrators of violence; they also have an important role as peace-makers. They are not so much the problem as at the heart of the solution.

186 Some of the most innovative programmes for involving young people in post-conflict reconstruction are provided by Commonwealth programmes themselves – an example is the project that explicitly seems to build respect and understanding among and between former child soldiers, young people and adults in the former conflict zone of Northern Uganda.

187 More generally, Commonwealth programmes provide examples of how young people's presence and skills can be valued, appreciated and used in activities normally undertaken only by adults. The Commonwealth Youth Programme engages young people in its own governance structures whilst youth representatives are included as members of election observation missions.

188 Other programmes focus on working alongside stigmatised groups. Groups in society with illnesses or diseases that are seen as a social taboo are often at the harsh end of casual, and sometimes even official, vilification and hatred. Their treatment amounts to an especially offensive form of disrespect, particularly if their original ailment or suffering is the product of poverty, hardship and ignorance.

Youth Ambassadors for Positive Living

189 Respect and understanding for people living with AIDS is promoted through a 'Youth Ambassadors for Positive Living' programme, operating in Africa, Asia and the Caribbean. The Youth Ambassadors are usually HIV-positive volunteers who engage in peer education and campaign for appropriate policy responses among government and civil society. Their message is one of de-stigmatisation.

190 One of the future activities planned is to develop learning materials for political literacy. The aim would be to enhance the capacity of organised youth groups and others to become effective advocates for democracy and good governance through their participation in observer missions, peace-building initiatives and other governance processes. This is very much in the mould of building resilience to extremism.

191 These are just a few of many examples. The challenge is to broaden and extend the effective participation of young women and men in the development process in their own countries and regions.

Empowerment can be created through youth parliaments

192   In the Pan-Commonwealth Youth Caucus, as well as in the overall youth sector in the Pacific Islands region, there is much discussion surrounding the need for countries to host annual or bi-annual Youth Parliaments to promote good governance through positive practice. Youth Parliaments, of which there are several models throughout the world, are exercises in which young people elect their own leaders and participate in a two-week parliamentary debate on issues of their choosing. The resolutions are then passed on to relevant government departments, the national legislative assembly and donors for consideration and further action.

193   The Tonga Youth Parliament is aiming to promote good governance through a different method in the near future. Rather than only electing young leaders, the Tonga National Youth Congress, with assistance from the Pacific Islands Forum Secretariat (PIFS), will train these leaders to behave with a level of respect appropriate to members of a national legislative assembly. When the young people act in a more respectful way, the expectation is that they will influence not only other young leaders but the national legislative assembly as well. The entire Youth Parliament is televised live and is also aired on the radio throughout all of the islands.

Sport can also promote empowerment and mutual understanding

194   The Commonwealth Games, perhaps one of the most visible and well-known aspects of the Commonwealth, are another good example of how the Commonwealth already promotes respect and understanding. Also known as the 'friendly games', the Games promote the pursuit of health and provide an opportunity for young people to strive for excellence, more so since the inauguration of the four-yearly Commonwealth Youth Games in 2000.

195   Sport is a vocation open to all people, irrespective of disability, ethnicity or economic position. Rigorous training and a commitment to winning medals for one's nation can help to overcome any perceived divides within that nation. The impact of the Games goes beyond the quadrennial event. In its commitment to the three core values of humanity, equality and destiny, the Commonwealth Games Federation also seeks to improve the lives and societies of Commonwealth people by assisting education through sport development and physical recreation.[xxiii]

xxiii   See www.thecgf.com

Education is inevitably central to the cause of respect and understanding

196 In the longer run, the biggest gains in shaping shared narratives across potential divides will most likely come from investment in, and rethinking of, education. This was one of the most frequently mentioned channels through which respect and understanding could be engendered that was identified by the Commission and by the high-level submissions made to the work of the Commission.

197 Thinking strategically about education, and especially about *how* to deliver education as a suitable intervention means several different things. It is helpful to break these down:

- *Educational participation* itself can be an important symptom of embedded inequality and lack of opportunity. The distribution of education shapes tendencies towards inclusion or exclusion and, thus, general patterns that are evident in a particular society. The effects on respect and understanding can be substantial, although they may be indirect in their nature. Policymakers are faced with the job of developing mechanisms to widen and deepen educational participation as a means of (a) overcoming societal tendencies to exclusion and/or (b) compensating for the injustice and/or barriers experienced by a particular group.

- *Extending the age 'reach'* of the compulsory schooling system upwards and downwards – and implementing this effectively – is extremely important. So also is extending participation in basic education in rural communities. The use of pioneering programmes to preserve household income generated through informal child working, whilst delivering a core education programme, is another important way of extending educational participation. The 'who' aspects of education are therefore central.

- *Educational content* is linked with the promotion of respect and understanding – or the opposite. Thus the educational curriculum is central in embodying and communicating values and messages about the relationships and understandings between and across existing identity groups. Teaching children in the compulsory schooling system about the cultural heritage of a range of ethnic and religious communities is a typical intervention based on multicultural models of stimulating appetite for knowledge. As well as giving an understanding of comparative religion and ethnic and cultural groups, it is important to teach children that there are fundamental human values that transcend religion, cultural and ethnic boundaries – the duty to treat others with respect and dignity, and to do unto others as you wish to be treated yourself.

198 Knowledge of world history is particularly critical in helping to forge cosmopolitan identities. Equally, teaching children about the value and purpose of social cohesion based on mutual equality is another, rather more ambitious intervention. Finally,

teaching can develop a range of ways to transfer knowledge in plural societies. Softer aspects of education are also relevant in relation to smoothing the adaptation of immigrants to their host or new home societies. The 'what' aspects of education are at the heart of all of these interventions.

- *Educational contributions* to the larger task of managing difference are important. The extent to which education plays a positive role in engendering respect for difference depends on how it is framed and used in a social context. Canadian bi-lingualism policies, for example, seek to go beyond expanding language usage and also offer an alternative way to think about education for all communities, irrespective of their particular identities or lines of heritage. Education in this sense is very much about preparing young – or younger – minds to live in and cope effectively with a world of various pluralisms.

199 Education is also an instrument for understanding both difference and the potential for fault-lines to descend into conflict and violence. At its most effective, education can be used to reflect on and gain a better understanding of conflict itself, insofar as knowledge can be conveyed in a way that shows that every major conflict involves an interaction between economic, political, historical and cultural factors and that in many cases, group mobilisation occurs along lines of ethnic, religious or ideological identity, which destroys ties of respect and understanding and replaces them with fear and mistrust. The 'how' aspects of education's role in shaping much larger social cohesion lie at the heart of this kind of educational approach and one interesting example, in a context where the majority of children are still educated in faith-related schools, is the Northern Ireland Education for Mutual Understanding initiative, which has been incorporated as a curriculum requirement.

200 The question of the renewal of the Commonwealth itself cannot be lightly dismissed in the context of education. Such renewal is possible only when we are able to discover and to keep re-discovering who we really are, how our lives have been forged from that textured history of hundreds of years, of which both the idea of Pax Britannica and the Commonwealth are also products.

201 Education is not just about school and college education, it is about life-long learning, including in very particular situations. Thus, for example, it includes programmes that aim to bring conflicting parties together in peace-building activities or in political education programmes in post-conflict situations.

202 Young people can and do play a role here, including as advisers and trainers. 'Education' also includes providing training support for young people to engage in and participate in governance processes – in youth organisations, trade unions, National Youth Councils and Parliaments. The Commonwealth Youth Programme has a large number of innovative programmes that encourage youth participation in a variety of functions; all seek to both inform and empower young people.

203   The Commission attaches importance to *quality*, relevant education, regardless of whether that education is provided by the state or not. In many countries, the non-government educational system has increased exponentially in response to lack of government resources to equip and staff government schools adequately (including valuing and remunerating teachers in ways that ensures their attendance). Bangladesh is perhaps one of the most interesting examples of this, with enormous investments by the NGO sector in children's and adult (particularly women's) education. The role of government then changes to one of providing a policy and regulatory framework, through which it can exert influence over wider educational objectives.

204   The Commission concluded that state policies that actively promote new faith schools, whether they are Christian, Jewish, Muslim or Hindu, may be problematic if the impact of these schools is that students learn to see the world in fragmented terms, with their faith identity setting them apart from others with different faiths or no faith at all. The proliferation of faith schools today comes at a time when prioritising religion in particular ways has been a major contributory factor to violence in many parts of the world. It is important, therefore, to insist that education is:

> '…not just about getting children, even very young ones, immersed in an old, inherited ethos. It is also about helping children to develop the ability to reason about new decisions that any grown-up person will have to take…and enhance (their) capability…to live "examined lives" as they grow up in an integrated country.' [xxiv]

205   Whether faith or secular, public or private, the emphasis must be on providing a high-quality, rounded education that encourages respect between all peoples and does not put forward the idea that any one dogma is pre-eminent. Faith schools are able to deliver this objective, so long as blinkered dogma is not the lens for their students.

206   There is a need for all countries to look at the totality of their education systems, both as sources of current marginalisation but also as sources of huge potential to help overcome that marginalisation. Education is paramount in the process of promoting respect and understanding between people, and particularly the young – the leaders, followers, thinkers and doers of the future. What they are taught and how they are taught is critical.

207   The Commission emphasises the critical role of education, defined in its broadest sense, in engendering a feeling of respect and understanding amongst diverse populations and particularly the young. The organisations that deliver these different educational programmes are as simple as school systems and as high-level as Commonwealth forums.

---

xxiv   Sen 2006, 160.

Chapter 8: Multilateralism and the International Order

A way of thinking and acting

208   The challenges of global violence and hatred are by no means new to governments and the international community. One of the core insights provided by its work is that one-sided imposed solutions have tended to fail in carrying hearts and minds, and that therefore such approaches are unlikely to be effective or credible.

209   The task is to arrive at an approach or style of engagement that is effective and credible precisely because the measures required can be sustained over a long period. Credibility accrues from having to build and nurture coalitions of interest, having to take into account the opinions of others, having to keep open lines of communication, and from affording respect to those of different views and values. The issue of effectiveness requires asking the simple question: does an intervention that is unilaterally imposed actually work in achieving its stated goals?

210   We have focused very heavily in this report on the need for more economically advanced countries to deal respectfully and with understanding in their relationships with other states, but it is important to point out that this is a two-way process. It is also the case that poorer countries must deal fairly with the more economically advanced countries. There are some leaders who dismiss all efforts by new leaders in these economically advanced countries to change and improve relationships. They wish to hold the new generation to account in perpetuity for all the misdeeds of history. Such snubs and rebuffs to those in the less economically advanced world who do wish to build respect and understanding is likely to be very counter-productive for all concerned. Respect and understanding is a process of mutuality.

211   These then are some of the hallmarks of a positive and constructive multilateral approach. They have substantial value in helping governments and others to address grievance and humiliation in order to curb violence and hatred. The Commonwealth itself is deeply imbued with this approach and its underlying philosophy of engagement. And, indeed, the Commission itself has carried out its task at the behest of a multilateral organisation. This necessarily implies a particular way of looking at, and thinking about, problems and arriving at better, shared solutions.

Multilateralism and unilateralism

212   Acting multilaterally has many advantages and these should be recalled at the outset:

- Multilateralism amounts to a way of looking at things in a rounded and balanced manner, with a sensitivity to the true complexities of the international problems faced by countries today.

- More often that not, the international order is more effectively served by, and geared to, this approach than to Big Power politics. Few, if any, powerful countries can act to preserve their interests alone. Even Big Powers implicitly, and explicitly through their membership of international organisations like the UN and Commonwealth and accession to international instruments, accept the case for working with others to secure their own interests and international order.

- The complexity of many current and emerging international issues is suited to a multilateral approach. This is because many of these issues embody the collective interests and responsibilities of all countries or of a group. Examples might be neighbours sharing a common resource or affected by a particular event, or facing a common environmental challenge, or a disparate group with a common interest such as economic vulnerability.

213   The Commission recognises that there may be situations in which unilateral action may be required and is permissible under international law, for example, self defence or in defence of a nation's citizens. However, even in cases where unilateral intervention has been required, or has taken place, it is striking to observe in many cases that there was a continuing need for multilateral tools to promote dialogue and afford dignity in reaching a solution. The latter may become small yet essential tests of the willingness of the powerful to engage with, and respond positively to, the interests and perspectives of the less powerful. There is a need to find answers which address the concerns and hopes of all parties, and this means that any approach where one side has a 'winner takes all' attitude is unlikely to be credible or effective.

214   The Commonwealth approach of dialogue and consensus building, in which even the least powerful member must be fully consulted, is an important example of this inherently multilateral approach. And as all members use the English language, communication can be both more efficient and more informal. As a result, the Commonwealth can use the power of language as a mechanism for protecting not only civil liberties, but also cultural rights.

215   South Africa stands out as perhaps the most striking example of the Commonwealth approach in action. Even when the country withdrew from the organisation in the early 1960s, the Commonwealth, rather than forsaking South Africa, made it a centrepiece of its activity. First it set out the position of principle, clearly defined in the condemnation of Apartheid and racism in the 1971 Singapore Principles. Then it moved to concrete actions such as sporting and economic sanctions, grappling with differences between member states in finding a broadly supported approach. At the same time it pushed the boundaries for engagement, highlighted by the 1985 Eminent Persons Group mission to South Africa. Then in the early 1990s it supported the internal negotiating process which led in 1994 to a free multi-racial South Africa and its return not only to Commonwealth membership, but Commonwealth leadership, with its hosting of the 1999 Durban CHOGM.

216   In the course of this, South Africa itself has become something of a model for a
       'rainbow nation', with mechanisms to address past grievance and some of the strongest
       protections of individual and community rights in the world.

217   More recently, in the last decade in Nigeria and Sierra Leone the Commonwealth rallied
       round to support the people of these nations as they faced up to military dictatorships.
       In the case of Sierra Leone, members co-operated with military as well as political
       support to see the legitimate government of President Kabbah returned. But in both
       cases, the crucial Commonwealth role came in the peace-building phase which followed
       democratic elections, when they worked with a wide range of international partners to
       support these members as they reclaimed civil government and grappled with the roots
       of past grievances. In both countries the Commonwealth-supported efforts continue.

218   These are familiar and credible examples of the multilateralist approach at work and
       bringing about concrete results. The outcomes have delivered benefits to all sides. And
       this is where the approach has direct relevance for today's conflicts. In some countries
       the approach has yielded greater freedoms for legitimate opposition parties and
       movements. In others, it has allowed greater inclusion of marginalised groups into the
       mainstream of society. And in yet others, it has spawned realistic and holistic strategies
       to combat terror.

219   It is this philosophy which also stands behind the Secretary-General's Good Offices
       work, to address potential causes of conflict and involve all parties in sustainable
       political and social solutions. In member nations as diverse as Guyana, Cameroon,
       Swaziland and Maldives these efforts have had considerable success and have been
       much appreciated by member governments. The Commission commends these Good
       Offices activities of the Commonwealth and the philosophy which inspires them as
       having a wide relevance for addressing grievance internationally, and acting as a model
       of multilateral support in support of the challenges faced by nations.

Late, though not lost, opportunities

220   It must be acknowledged that this approach, slow and consultative by nature, is not
       always immediately successful. Zimbabwe, which has withdrawn from the
       Commonwealth, is a case in point. In Zimbabwe, the absence of a viable political
       solution acceptable to all sides that also addresses longstanding grievances, as well as
       a failure to meet Commonwealth concerns and expectations, remains a major concern.
       But this absence should not be taken to infer that such an outcome cannot yet be
       attained by the use of a Commonwealth, multilateralist approach. The South African
       case gives hope for a way forward. By going with the grain of the approach outlined
       here, the Commission desperately hopes that a successful outcome in Zimbabwe
       remains within reach. The current situation is a cruel and unnecessary tragedy for the
       people of Zimbabwe.

221   This approach may also have something to offer in the current vexed context of Iraq, where there are growing calls for greater multilateral engagement. It can be argued that the escalation of violence in Iraq under occupation following recent elections illustrates the penalties of a singular concentration on voting (the illusion that 'if there are elections we have a functioning democracy'), since democratic political processes often require public discussion, including addressing new divisions as well as the history of past tensions and conflicts. There is a great need to ensure a political and security climate in which public discussion without barriers of community divisions can proceed. The international community needs to help promote this public discussion.

222   Afghanistan's difficulties also represent a late, though not lost, opportunity for multilateralism, especially given the political commitment of the United Nations. The Afghan people underwent untold suffering over several decades of armed conflict, which was triggered by the invasion of Afghanistan by foreign troops. The Geneva Accords, signed in 1988, entrusted the UN with a monitoring role and the expectation that Afghanistan would thus be restored to its people, and a multi-ethnic democracy would be set up. This expectation remains unrealised, as externally supported inter-ethnic conflict prevents the restoration of peace and the return home of large numbers of refugees and displaced persons. Afghanistan has in effect become an abandoned state. The UN Strategic Framework for Afghanistan statement prepared in September 1998 described the desperate reality of Afghanistan thus:

> 'It mixes a volatile and violent political crisis, a human rights and humanitarian emergency, and two decades of missed development opportunities. The fragmentation of the country and the collapse of practically all institutions of the State, also constitute "an emergency of governance".' [xxv]

223   The Commission believes that a multilateralist approach remains the most credible way forward. The 2001 Bonn Agreement contained the following core elements of a strategy to rescue and rebuild Afghanistan:

■ A process to be nurtured and facilitated by the UN which would involve all segments of the Afghan population and enable them to participate in the implementation of the framework and basis of lasting peace in Afghanistan.

■ A process of meaningful consultations to be sustained with all segments of the Afghan people in all parts of Afghanistan and those displaced outside the country.

■ The basic elements of the framework were: (a) recognition of the right to choose freely a broad-based, multi-ethnic and fully representative government consisting of representatives of all segments of the Afghan people; (b) an inclusive participatory process which would involve continuing consultations to spell out each phase of the transition and clearly formulated steps to be taken in each phase; (c) while this transition was being affected within the agreed framework, the international

---

xxv   Reproduced in Hossain 1999.

community would commit the needed resources to support the process of re-construction and in particular to the strategic goal of building capacity for providing national security.

224 The Commission believes that strong international engagement will continue to be required to address the remaining challenges. Unemployment, the large-scale revival of poppy cultivation, and the increasing insurgency of the Taliban are matters of grave concern. Therefore, a meaningful contribution can be made towards truly restoring Afghanistan to all of its peoples. This involves a resumption of the Commonwealth approach by the international community in order to reinstate genuine stability and democracy through development and the participation of people affected by violence and fragmentation. Respect and understanding among all the segments of the Afghan population must provide the foundation for a multi-ethnic and stable democracy.

225 Similar approaches and conclusions can be applied to other outstanding conflicts and trouble-spots within and beyond the Commonwealth:

- Combating extremism and terrorism requires governments to go beyond security and intelligence measures. Sustained solutions are most likely through multilateral co-operation to isolate and deplete support for extremist ideologies of hatred and fear.

- Unilateral military interventions, sometimes guided by humanitarian motives, are nevertheless dependent on securing political settlements rapidly in their wake. Failure to arrive at such a settlement risks returning to earlier cycles of violence and even escalation with greater turmoil and suffering.

- Long-standing opponents have, in some cases, been able to liberate themselves from a winner-takes-all mindset. Multilateralist thinking has been critical in doing so. In Northern Ireland, a peace dividend now combines with a security dividend with benefits for all.

Respect and understanding have to be carried to issues of injustice and the international order

226 At any moment in history, there are grievances that have to do with the perceived unfairness of the world system and the unjustly strident behaviour of powerful countries or blocs. The reasons for sentiments of injustice depend to a great extent on historical circumstance and the balance of power in that particular period – thus grievances experienced by people and countries during the Cold War have different geneses than grievances experienced today.

227 As with local-level conflicts conducted through the lens of identities, there is an initial tendency to explain feelings of global injustice primarily in economic terms. Some have argued that it is the lack of economic integration of Southern economies into the neo-liberal global economic system, which is the cause of social dislocation, and that the economic hegemony of Western countries has provoked Islamic militancy.

228   There is some basic logic in this argument. The extensive restructuring of the world system of production and division of labour during the past 20 years has generated unprecedented benefits for some regions, countries and individuals. However, the effects are highly uneven, including within countries.

229   Poorer countries have borne the brunt of demographic pressures. Migration, predominantly of young people, is one example. It is estimated that in 2005 there were over 191 million international migrants worldwide,[xxvi] the majority from developing countries. This has had a major negative impact on the skills base of developing countries. At the same time, in the receiving countries it tends to increase competition between disadvantaged groups as they struggle for jobs, housing and services. But more positively it has enormously increased the diversity of peoples in developed countries. Furthermore, remittances to developing countries as a result have contributed significantly to their capital inflows and community development. Although the persistence of high levels of poverty and unequal participation in international decision-making processes create a sense of being 'left behind' in the broad sweep of globalisation, there are also other factors operating.

The stark problem of double standards

230   The Commission concludes that a more significant issue – and one of the underlying causes of a deep sense of injustice in the world today – is not the economic hegemony of (largely) Western industrialised nations per se, but rather, the perception that some of these nations have created an environment where there are no rules based on international law, only national self-interest. This, then, plays into the hands of extremist groups with a grievance agenda:

> 'Organisations that employ terror have gained legitimacy by the often cynical, hypocritical and abusive exercise of power in the international realm by today's most developed democracies. Preaching the protection of rights at home, the military and intelligence organisations of the great powers have too often supported abusive regimes abroad if in doing so they gain strategic military advantage or access to natural resources'.[xxvii]

231   Instances of nations acting in this manner have long historical roots. Throughout the colonial period and during the Cold War, both Western governments and the Soviet Union supported proxy wars in third countries, particularly in Africa, Latin America and South-East Asia. Taking advantage of local grievances and conflict but often funded by outsiders, these wars subverted people's democratic rights and had devastating effects on the lives of all those caught up in them.

---

xxvi   UN DESA 2005, 1.

xxvii   Putzel 2005, 5.

232   Although the incidence of proxy wars has decreased since the end of the Cold War, the involvement of rich countries in armed conflicts in third states continues through the export of arms. Of the total exports of conventional arms in the world in 2006, as much as 79 per cent was sold by the five permanent members of the Security Council, and 80 per cent by the G8 countries, with many countries common to both lists.[xxviii]

233   If the average spent on arms every year had been put to the service of education and health in Africa, Asia, the Middle East and Latin America, it is estimated that every child could be in school and child mortality could be reduced by two-thirds – fulfilling two of the MDGs by 2015. Responsibility for the 'opportunity cost' of arms is that of buying countries, but also of the G8 nations.

234   In recent years, the perception of injustice and a failure to protect human rights in the conflict in the Middle East generally, and the Israeli–Palestinian conflict in particular, has been felt most acutely in the context of international law and the protection of human rights. The UN 'Alliance of Civilizations' report sees the Palestine issue as a major factor in the widening rift between Muslim-majority and Western societies. It identifies this as a – if not the – priority issue for resolution.

235   Although it is extremely difficult to attribute causality to the approach of some Western countries to particular conflicts, researchers consistently identify the prolonged Israeli–Palestinian conflict, the invasion of Iraq, and the continued presence of Western military forces there as important factors in the radicalisation of young Muslims, particularly those in Western countries. The Commission believes this needs to be addressed – and dialogue and consistency in action which conforms to agreed international standards is an important means of beginning to achieve this.

Engagement with and through international institutions, in itself, confers respect

236   A different sort of impunity occurs when powerful countries refuse to ratify, or, having ratified, refuse to honour, UN and other international agreements and treaties. Many countries are slow to follow through on their international commitments due to capacity constraints as well as for political reasons. There is, therefore, a pressing need for the world's most powerful countries and oldest democracies to show demonstrated commitment to this process.

237   The controversy over the treatment of prisoners at Guantanamo and Abu Ghraib has raised questions about respect for international law. The Commission believes that such incidents weaken the moral authority of the world's most economically advanced countries. Some argue it gives organisations advocating terror the opportunity to

xxviii   Grimmett 2006.

operate from what may be seen as the moral high ground, though in fact organisations that are committed to violence and extremism have forfeited the real moral high ground. The Commission observes that the outcomes are deeply damaging for Western developed countries and can permit terrorist and extremist organisations and groups bent on hatred and violence to gain tactical advantage in shaping hearts and minds.

Devaluing the currency of respect and understanding

238   A sense of injustice and unilateral invulnerability can have long-term consequences, particularly when they arise from actions which are undertaken by the world's most developed democracies. The effects of these actions are to erode trust between countries in various ways:

- They can create a precedent of rule-breaking that may be hard to contain.

- They may reduce support from other countries that no longer trust their integrity.

- There is evidence that they allow radical elements to gain legitimacy amongst a wider public.

239   If the world's developed democracies are seen to abuse their power, opt out of international agreements (such as on the environment), or act solely in their own perceived interests, it is possible that others will follow their lead. Individuals and groups must have a reason to trust in international systems of governance and see them as applying equally to all nations.

240   There is, in addition, a pressing need to respect decisions made by the people when they have been consulted in a credible way. Big power states are wrong-footed when they do not accept the decisions of the people as expressed through democratic elections. A particularly challenging case is one outside the Commonwealth – in Palestine. There, after demanding that all parties and groups submit to the democratic process, most Western governments refused to accept the electoral outcome. There is on the one hand, the need for all countries including the world leaders to accept the outcomes of free and fair elections, no matter where they occur, and also on the other hand, the need for elected parties to abide by the requirements of democratic processes, including respecting rights of other parties, media and open public discussion.

Respect and understanding to underpin change is embodied in Commonwealth membership as well

241   When countries have been suspended from the Commonwealth, it has normally been because they have been unable to honour the Commonwealth principle of dialogue and participatory freedom with regard to their own people. Thus suspension has been incurred where the military has overthrown democratically elected governments or where there have been serious or persistent violations of Commonwealth values.

242   But, significantly, it is not the Commonwealth approach to cut connections completely or to ask member countries to leave the Commonwealth family; when members leave it is normally their leaders' decision, as was the case with Zimbabwe. This is particularly tragic given the effort expended by the Commonwealth in supporting the people of Zimbabwe to achieve their freedom from the Rhodesian regime.

243   As is often the case in human relations, those who have been abused can become the abusers. The terrible violence being done to the opposition and many ordinary people in the country today, shows no respect for common humanity, the rule of law, or even self-interested economics. It is our belief that this is not because the Commonwealth way of working has failed, but rather that it has not been tried over the years with enough persuasion and persistence. The Commission acknowledges that efforts with regard to Zimbabwe continue, and must be strengthened.

Showing respect to regional neighbours reflects and reinforces multilaterist thinking

244   Deep feelings of disrespect and humiliation sometimes emanate from a feeling of how 'one's people' are being treated in other countries by other peoples and by other governments. In short, kith-and-kinship identity can become both regionalised and globalised. In searching for ways to re-engender feelings of respect and understanding at a local level, the Commission believes there is also need to understand this wider sense of injustice – to understand why it occurs and how it can be addressed.

245   True regional co-operation needs to be based on sentiments of respect and understanding between nations in the region, whatever the size of their economy or their political influence. A partnership approach is one outcome. Greater understanding between partners who take different views is another.

246   Small, landlocked countries are particularly reliant on relations with larger neighbours, as are small island states on the development of good regional networks and sound policies that benefit them all. Island states tend to have certain vulnerabilities in common: to environmental disasters, to the consequences of climate change, to the international trade system, and to public health issues, including HIV/AIDS. Sometimes they have the added difficulty of communicating within and between countries because of distance (the collections of islands that make up Kiribati stretch over 3,500km).

247   These factors mean that these small island states must develop partnerships, based on trust, for developing shared beneficial strategies, pooling their human and financial resources and establishing priorities. They have a lot to gain from close dialogue and co-operation with each other and with their larger neighbours.

248   Regional grievances are most likely to arise as a result of economically and politically dominant countries behaving in a way that makes smaller countries feel like periphery states. This can occur whenever there is a considerable discrepancy in scale. In the Pacific region, Australia and New Zealand are the strongest nations in terms of economic status and also the largest donors to other Pacific Islands. For the Caribbean the US is the dominant regional power.

249   Powerful countries need to be continually aware that there are thoughtful and respectful ways to conduct affairs with smaller neighbours. They also need to be motivated to act in accordance with their awareness. Principles of respect need to underlie all relationships, not just high-level ones between governments, but between the whole range of institutional and individual contacts that citizens and youth groups have with each other. Finally, and importantly, it means seeing small states as homelands to people, cultures and perspectives – and not primarily as potential problems, for example, as havens for terrorists.

250   Small states are integral to the Commonwealth's identity: as a diverse group of nations, 32 of its 53 member countries are small states, most of them with populations of less than 1.5 million. Small states are making determined efforts to pursue sustainable growth and devise coherent strategies for integrating their economies with the larger trading blocs and with new trading systems. The Commonwealth is supporting small states in these endeavours and is an excellent forum to emphasise the importance of all countries being treated with respect and as equals, regardless of the size of their economy, their population or their influence on world affairs.

Chapter 9: The Way Forward

Promoting dignity and dialogue

251   The Commonwealth Commission for Respect and Understanding was established in response to growing concerns about systematic group violence in the world, and the widespread disrespect and anger that prepare the ground for it. Antagonism and violence along the lines of exploitable divisions have taken on a global character in recent years. They find expression in acts of terrorism against civilian populations, and in violent confrontations over territories and entitlements. Even some of the military strategies to combat terror have made their own contributions to casualties, including that of civilian populations.

252   A meeting of the Heads of Governments of Commonwealth countries is a good occasion for discussing and coordinating public policies within the group which has greatly benefited in the past from such interactions. It is also an excellent opportunity to examine the state of the world and the problems that the Commonwealth countries share with other countries around the globe. Aside from its territorially confined functions, the Commonwealth is an important global player in an increasingly interdependent world, and it has a duty to do what it can in trying to solve shared problems across the globe. This report, therefore, is concerned not only with what can be called the 'home affairs' of the Commonwealth (that too, of course, very importantly, but not just that), but also with the Commonwealth's role in directing attention to policy issues of general interest in the world, across regional boundaries.

253   One of the principal points of concentration of this report is the need for more active multilateralism to address shared problems in our strife-ridden world. The Commonwealth, with its considerable background – and success – in using multilateral means, can have a very important influence in pressing for that important approach. Indeed, the focus on dialogue on the basis of acknowledgement of the dignity of all people has been a quintessential mode of operation in the Commonwealth – it is even tempting to call it 'the Commonwealth approach'. There is every reason, we argue in this report, to emphasise, rather than renounce, this well-used approach in addressing the gigantic problems of peace and security that the world faces today.

254   Efforts to defeat terrorism call for a clear-headed understanding of the nature of contemporary group violence. It is possible to argue that the limited achievements, and sometimes counterproductive results, of well-meant initiatives to further peace in the world are closely linked with deficiencies in the underlying readings of the nature and genesis of global violence. Since the consequences, for example in Iraq, seem to have surprised and disappointed even some of the earlier advocates of these policies, the time for rethinking is surely now; all countries, irrespective of their past policies, should have a strong interest in this process. Even when past policies have achieved, at least

initially, considerable success, for example in Afghanistan, the follow-up events have revealed serious difficulties that call for diagnostic analysis of what should have been done differently.

255   The Commonwealth has a long tradition of learning from critical examinations of its past policies, and the history of the Commonwealth is a testament to the importance of open-mindedness in undertaking retrospective scrutiny for prospective improvement. As it happens, even at the time when some of the more debatable campaigns were launched, there were also other readings of contemporary events – very different from those that inspired the campaigns – that were also defended in other quarters in the world, many of them within the Commonwealth countries themselves. Paying fuller attention to the wealth of understanding that existed then, could have, quite possibly, helped in a better-informed pursuit of world peace and security. Efforts in search of peace can, in fact, be ineffective and counterproductive if they are based on a deficient appreciation of the underlying nature of global conflicts. The scrutiny that genuinely multilateral consultations and interactions can provide has pervasive importance and usefulness in determining the appropriate means for pursuing peace and security.

Conclusion 1: Use of Dialogue and Multilateralism

256   The Commonwealth has a well-established approach to tackling conflict and political differences, involving multilateral consultations and extensive dialogues, even when the positions held by different parties seem distant. In a world in which different people, despite sharing a common interest in peace, security and justice, find themselves divided by mutual incomprehension and scepticism, and sometimes even suspicion, the affirmation of the importance of multilateralism, with mutual respect, can help to create a more positive climate for toleration, support and collaboration. We attach great importance to the Commonwealth's role in placing constructive emphasis on the use of a dialogue-based approach to dealing with issues of group-based conflict in the world today.

257   More particularly, we urge the Commonwealth to use its considerable successful experience to contribute to mobilising the international community, working with and within the United Nations and other international organisations. There is, we argue, a strong need for doing what we can to ensure that channels of dialogue remain open, that there are discussions to identify common platforms, that shared interests and concerns receive general attention, and that potential flashpoints are identified and addressed.

258   In the half decade following 9/11, global support for, and identification with, the US as victims of an extreme outrage has shifted undeniably. A large part of the general attitude has moved towards irritation, sometimes even hostility, in relation to the US-led strategy. It is instructive to examine why this has happened, and what could have

been done to prevent it. A greater use of multilateralism and the policy differences that this would have made are natural candidates to examine in answering these questions. The Commonwealth can play a hugely constructive role in the world today in bringing to the fore the importance of multilateralism and the effectiveness of a dialogue-based *modus operandi* in dealing with issues related to violent conflict.

Conclusion 2: Commitment to Civil Paths — Not to be Displaced by Military Initiatives

259   Commonwealth governments can help to promote a better understanding of the far-reaching implications of the general recognition that tackling global terrorism is far more than a security problem. Aside from governmental initiatives, civil society organisations can also play a constructive role here. The recognition that terrorism is more than a security problem is by no means novel in the world, but its bearing on the choice of policy priorities has been considerably eclipsed by the recent focus on military options and strong-armed security measures. Probing and robust policing is certainly very important in preventing terrorist activities. And yet terrorism has many complex underlying factors. Security policies, while generally important, cannot on their own, come anywhere close to solving – or even suppressing – the problems of terrorism. Many of these problems have to be more fully addressed through civil means, in addition to what the security procedures can achieve.

260   The recruitment of terrorist activists and the creation of a climate where violent deeds are tolerated by a large section of a normally peaceful population undoubtedly rely on impassioned advocacies of violence and emotional evocation of some special group identity, to the exclusion of all other affiliations. There is a need for much more dialogue and discussion on the richness of human identities and also on the need to avoid placing people in rigidly separated boxes, linked with religion or community. The cultivation of a non-denominational national identity can also be very important in providing political cohesion within a country, without denying the claims of broader identities that people may also wish to pursue, linked with continental loyalties (such as Europe, Asia, Africa or the Caribbean), or even the shared human identity that all enjoy. Policies here have to pay particular attention to the nature and content of school education, as well as public discussion. The avoidance of sectarian divisions within a nation can be a very important component of the civil approach to peace, and the positive features of a non-divisive national political identity need, right now, a clear and ungrudging recognition.

261   The civil paths must also include addressing past – or present – humiliations, and what is widely seen as continued 'injustice' at the expense of the less-privileged parts of humanity. Extremism and radical search for violent 'solutions' operate through various alliances with those who have reasoned complaints about the nature of the world in which we all live.

262   We live in a world that has come to be dominated by military actions and violent encounters, where even those who are opposed to such methods tend to concentrate almost entirely on the counterproductive nature of the violent routes to peace, rather than on the positive and constructive role of civil initiatives. The Commonwealth can greatly serve the world, in addition to itself, in bringing the civil paths very strongly in focus for public policy across the world, including of course in the Commonwealth countries themselves. What is particularly needed now is not so much a detailed 'civilian manifesto', but a firm recognition of the necessary role of civil routes to peace and security. Very few things are as important today, we argue, as this general understanding and affirmation.

Conclusion 3: Addressing grievance and humiliation

263   Among the civil initiatives, particular importance has to be attached to those policies that promote the understanding and remedying of the underlying causes of grievance. In defeating terrorism, the perceived sense of grievances demands serious attention. When there is some basis for complaints, the case for corresponding institutional reform can be strong. The reach and effectiveness of that civil approach can be illustrated with the success of the visionary Scarman Report in 1982,[xxix] led by Lord Scarman in Britain, which greatly helped in overcoming the hostilities that found expression in race-related riots in 1981 in Brixton and Birmingham. Such riots have not returned in Britain since then, although similar ones have occurred elsewhere.

264   And when, as is sometimes the case, the confrontational perceptions are based on confusion or planted through extremist instigation, those misapprehensions would still have to be addressed through civil means, with good use of discussion, open scrutiny and a willingness on the part of others to listen to complaints and grievances.

265   Good use can be made of the experience of the Truth and Reconciliation Commission in South Africa. Its mode of operation included the need for the government both to acknowledge the perspective of the aggrieved, with detailed factual records, and also to make room for the burying of past hostilities when the inherited inequities are properly addressed in the present.[xxx]

266   The outcomes of these changes would have to be periodically evaluated, in a systematic way, since long-standing problems are not amenable to a 'once and for all' eradication. These evaluations should include tangible ways in which the perspective of aggrieved groups receives an airing and commands attention. And yet progress must ultimately be judged by the gradual elimination of the sense of grievance, both (1)

xxix   Scarman 1981.

xxx   Mani 2002.

through remedying measures, and when necessary, institutional reforms, and (2) through addressing perceptions of inequity with genuine interest and concern. While detailed plans would have to be worked out in the light of specific circumstances in each country (we have presented some possible ways and means to consider in different chapters of the report), the general strategy of going in this direction has to be clearly recognised and affirmed.

Conclusion 4: Political participation and inclusion

267   If participation is an important part of a multilateral approach to world peace, the critical role of political participation within the borders of a country can hardly be overemphasised. While this recognition is hard to escape, its far-reaching implications often receive inadequate attention.

268   There is, first of all, the importance of a national identity that allows each citizen (and broadly even residents) of a country to participate in the political affairs of an undivided nation, as equals. The political sense of belonging to a nation need not be mediated through a person's religious or cultural identity: they have, of course, their own domain of relevance in other activities, like worship and the conduct of private lives and social intercourse. A national identity can be used to give each person an acknowledged equality in political participation, irrespective of religion, race, caste or community. Peace and the avoidance of violence within the borders of a country are very dependent on the cultivation of a non-divisive national identity – necessary for civil participation in the affairs of the country – without undermining the broader political or social identities that people also have across those borders.

269   The development of civil society is another area to which special attention has to be paid. While 'faith groups' are often well organised and well financed (sometimes from abroad), the non-religious identities, linked with language, literature, occupation, etc., have frequently been eclipsed by the increased role of religious politics in recent years. (For example, secular Bangladeshis in London often complain that their voice has been reduced both by the activities of faith groups and by the official priority given to religion over language in classifying the immigrant population.) The variety of groupings needs support, rather than dissuasion, since the diversity of groups helps to bring neglected concerns to public attention.

270   There is a delicate issue of leadership in pursuing the activism of civil society. There is much evidence to indicate that leadership can be very important in championing unpopular causes. Leadership can come from different groups of concerned as well as aggrieved people, including grassroots activists. Political leaders who draw attention to inequality and neglect may require special support, despite the worry that sometimes arises in the minds of the guardians of law and order. However, vocal but peaceful

political participation can have the dual role of (1) leading to a more informed making of public policy, and (2) removing discontent about not being heard, which can ultimately contribute to rage and violence.

Conclusion 5: Women's Political Participation

271 It is particularly important to pay special attention to women's political participation, since this is often seriously neglected. In this field, the Commonwealth has quite a wealth of initiatives and experiences, from which the different countries can benefit.

272 We have suggested particular procedures for making better use of the ties of the Commonwealth for this purpose, including:

1. the use of cross-Commonwealth measures of participation of women in electoral politics, both as candidates and as voters;

2. development of training and exchange programmes for women politicians, and aspiring entrants, to share experiences and lessons across different Commonwealth countries;

3. use of findings of research identifying particular barriers to political participation that women experience in different countries, and addressing the difficulties in the light of experiences in other countries; and

4. sharing of models of successful incorporation of women into civic and political life.

Conclusion 6: Contributions of the Media and Communication

273 A flourishing media can make a very large contribution in strengthening the civil paths to peace and security. Since governments are often tempted to restrain the press for one reason or another, the overall importance of a free media does need a firm acknowledgement. A flourishing media can make public discussion better informed, allow alternative points of view to be more fully expressed, and also help make the shared objectives of the nation and the world more analysed and understood. In our chapter dealing with the media (Chapter 6), we have proposed a number of specific policies, dealing with both traditional means and new methods of communication, but in addition, it is extremely important to recognise the role of an unrestrained and flourishing media in helping political participation and dialogue, allowing grievances to be aired and addressed, and facilitating the hearing that public appreciation and complaints should receive.

274   This is not to deny that there are cases in which the media has been used to generate hostility to others and to promote violence. While some restraints would, thus, be useful and sometimes necessary, particular care has to be taken to make sure that the steps to do this are proportionate and balanced so as to safeguard the survival and health of legitimate free expression, which is central to the civil paths to peace and security. It is always best if self-restraint is undertaken out of a sense of professional and social responsibility rather than the restraints having to be imposed externally.

Conclusion 7: Education and the role of young people

275   In the civil paths to peace and security, it would be hard to exaggerate the importance of non-sectarian and non-parochial education that expand, rather than reduce, the reach of understanding and reason. We have discussed, in Chapter 7, a number of specific policy proposals that would help the Commonwealth countries to learn from each other's experience.

276   Commonwealth governments do, of course, recognise that young people are the inheritors of global change. This recognition has two different implications. First, it is important to understand the contribution of young people which is already enriching contemporary politics and social practice – one type of illustration comes from the use of 'YouTube', but there are many other types of constructive initiatives as well. Second, the understanding that today's young people will have serious responsibility for the future, which in turn has implications for policies that try to help the young people of today to acquire the skill, efficiency and inclination to play active roles in shaping solutions to problems that they will have to deal with in the future. Nothing perhaps is as important here as making young people appreciate each other's dignity, despite their diversity, and also the importance of the creative functions of dialogue and discussion.

A concluding remark

277   This report has been informed by the importance of human minds in the pursuit of peace and security. This does not, in any way, underestimate the relevance of more standard thinking on the subject of war and peace. Military operations can, sometimes, be justified, and security measures are certainly extremely important in the prevention of violence and in the sustaining of peace. And yet it is the battle for human minds on which the successes and failures of terrorism ultimately depend.

278   Systematically 'engineered violence' makes effective – and often lethal – use of selected group identities with adversarial attitudes towards other groups, combined with the downplaying of many other identities that human beings also have, including the broad commonality of our shared humanity. In resisting engineered violence, we need as clear an understanding as possible of the ways and means through which the

thinking of a large number of activists is influenced in a violent direction. The battle for the human mind is at least as important in resisting terrorism and brutality as battles to secure physical bridgeheads.

279   This should not be a difficult point to appreciate, given the manifest nature of global violence and terrorism, including the way the process of recruitment works from the potential catchment population, and the way widespread frustrations and grievances are used to build up a favourable climate for violence, with tolerance of violent deeds (often seen as 'retaliatory violence'). But difficult or not, the practical implications of the point have not received the attention they strongly deserve. Our concentration has been to bring out with clarity the implications of this general understanding.

280   Given the nature of the subject matter, some of our conclusions are more general than others, with recommendation of an approach, particularly the use of multilateralism and the Commonwealth's well established method of dialogue with recognition of mutual dignity. We have requested the Secretary-General to develop concrete steps that, depending on their specific circumstances, member governments might find helpful to consider. The Commission urges member countries to examine carefully these suggestions as developed.

281   While precise policies must depend on specific circumstances and vary from country to country, the Commission wants to emphasise the overwhelming importance of agreeing on some general policy priorities at the present time. This is exactly where the Commonwealth, with its history and experience of dialogue, multilateralism and civil initiatives can play a critically important role. There is something of importance here that remains very pertinent and useful for the Commonwealth itself, but which also has, we have argued, very wide relevance for other countries as well. The Commonwealth does have something to offer to our troubled and fierce world, in addition to having reason to reaffirm its own commitments and to making fuller use of them in working for peace with dignity.

References

Appiah, Kwame Anthony (2005) *The Ethics of Identity.* Princeton University Press, Princeton, NJ.

_____(2006). *Cosmopolitanism: Ethics in a World of Strangers* Norton, New York.

Clarke, Charles (2006) 'Global citizens and quality international education: Enlarging the role of the Commonwealth'. Speech delivered to the Royal Commonwealth Society, 15 November, 2006, London.

Estlund, Cynthia (2003) *Working Together: How Workplace Bonds Strengthen a Diverse Democracy.* Oxford University Press, New York.

Gregorios, Archbishop of Thyateira and Great Britain (2007) 'Submission to the Commonwealth Commission on Respect and Understanding, 7 February, 2007'.

Grimmett, Richard F. (2006) 'Conventional Arms Transfers to Developing Nations, 1998–2005'. The Library of Congress, Congressional Research Service, 2006. Available for download from the Stockholm International Peace Research Institute: http://www.sipri.org/contents/armstrad/CRS_DevNat_1998-05.pdf/download (Last Accessed 8 August, 2007)

Hossain, Kamal (1999) 'Question of the violation of human rights and fundamental freedoms in any part of the world: Report of the situation of human rights in Afghanistan' submitted by Mr Kamal Hossain, Special Rapporteur, in accordance with Commission on Human Rights resolution 1998/70. Commission on Human Rights, United Nations. E/CN.4/1999/40 24 March, 1999.

Malik, M. (2005) 'Discrimination, equality and community cohesion', in *Muslims in the UK: Policies for Engaged Citizens.* Open Society Institute, Budapest.

Mani, Rama (2002) *Beyond Retribution: Seeking Justice in the Shadows of War.* Polity Press, Malden.

Moskos, Charles (1986) 'Success Story: Blacks in the Military', *The Atlantic.* Vol.257, No.5, pp.64-72.

National Crime Records Bureau, Government of India, Delhi (2006) *Crime in India 2005.* Table 1.8.

Plummer, David and L. Irwin (2006) 'Grassroots activities, national initiatives and HIV prevention: What explains Australia's dramatic early success in controlling the HIV epidemic?'. *International Journal of STI & AIDS* 17(12): 787–793.

Putzel, J (2005) 'Globalisation, liberalisation and prospects for the state', *International Political Science Review* Vol.26, No.1: 5–16.

Royal Commonwealth Society (2007) 'Submission to the Commonwealth Commission on Respect and Understanding, 16 February, 2007'.

Scarman, Leslie George, Baron (1981) 'The Brixton disorders 10–12 April 1981: Report of an enquiry'. Cmnd 8427. HMSO, London.

Sen, Amartya (1998) 'Human Rights: Is there a Commonwealth perspective?'. First Commonwealth Lecture, delivered 7 May, 1998, London.

_____(1999) 'Reason before Identity: Romanes Lecture 1998'. Oxford University Press, Oxford.

_____(2006) *Identity and Violence: The Illusion of Destiny.* Norton, New York and Penguin, London.

Stewart, F. (2005) 'Policies towards Horizontal Inequalities in Post-Conflict Reconstruction'. Centre for Research on Inequality, Human Security and Ethnicity (CRISE), Working Paper 7. Queen Elizabeth House, University of Oxford.

Taylor, Charles (2007). Winner of the Templeton Prize for 'Progress Toward Research or Discoveries About Spiritual Realities', 14 March, 2007.

Tevoedjre, Albert (2002) *Winning the War Against Humiliation.* Report of the Independent Commission on Africa and the challenges of the Third Millennium. UNDP Cotonou.

United Nations Department of Economic and Social Affairs (2004) *Social Dimensions of International Migration.* United Nations, New York.

_____(2005) *Trends in Total Migrant Stock: The 2005 Revision.* United Nations, New York.

United Nations Development Fund for Women (UNIFEM) Annual Report 2000

United Nations Development Fund for Women (UNIFEM) Annual Report 2004– 2005

United Nations Development Fund for Women (UNIFEM) Annual Report 2006–2007

Appendix A: Members of the Commonwealth Commission on Respect and Understanding

Professor Amartya Sen (India) – Chairperson - is Lamont University Professor and Professor of Economics and Philosophy at Harvard University. Until recently he was the Master of Trinity College, Cambridge. He has served as President of the Econometric Society, the Indian Economic Association, the American Economic Association and the International Economic Association. He formerly served as Honorary President of OXFAM and is now its Honorary Advisor. Born in India, Sen studied at Presidency College and at Trinity College. His previous posts include the Drummond Professor of Political Economy at Oxford University, and Professor of Economics at Delhi University and at the London School of Economics. Among the awards Amartya Sen has received are the Bharat Ratna (the highest honour awarded by the President of India), the Eisenhower Medal, the George C. Marshall Award, the Brazilian Ordem do Merito Cientifico (gra-Cruz), Companion of Honour (UK), the Edinburgh Medal, and the Nobel Prize in Economics. His most recent book is *Identity and Violence*, published by Norton and Penguin.

Rt Hon. Lord John Alderdice (United Kingdom)
John, Lord Alderdice (United Kingdom) was from 1987 to 1998 leader of Northern Ireland's cross-community Alliance Party, and played a key role in the negotiation of the 1998 Belfast Agreement. He was the first Speaker of the new Northern Ireland Assembly from 1998 until 2004, and was then appointed as one of four international monitoring commissioners overseeing security normalisation in Ireland. He sits on the Liberal Democrat benches in the House of Lords, and since 2005 has been the elected President of Liberal International - the world-wide federation of liberal political parties. He runs the Centre for Psychotherapy in Belfast and is a Visiting Professor in Psychiatry and Joint Chairman of the Critical Incident Analysis Group at the University of Virginia, with a special interest in the psychology of terrorism and violent political conflict.

Professor Kwame Anthony Appiah (Ghana) is Laurence S. Rockefeller University Professor of Philosophy and the University Center for Human Values at Princeton University. He has published widely in African and African-American literary and cultural studies, and in 1992, Oxford University Press published *In My Father's House*, which deals, in part, with the role of African and African-American intellectuals in shaping contemporary African cultural life. His most recent publications include *The Ethics of Identity* (2004) and *Cosmopolitanism: Ethics in a World of Strangers* (2006).

Rt Hon. Adrienne Clarkson (Canada) is an accomplished journalist and until 2005 she served as the 26th Governor General of Canada: she was the first Chinese Canadian and second woman to hold this position. She was also the first (and thus far only) Governor General to be awarded the Order of Canada prior to taking office. Clarkson is well known for her work in broadcasting, having hosted and produced several shows for the CBC between 1964 and 1982.

Dr Noeleen Heyzer (Singapore) is the first executive director from the South to head the United Nations Development Fund for Women (UNIFEM), the leading operational agency within the United

Nations to promote women's empowerment and gender equality. She played a critical role in the Security Council's adoption of Resolution 1325 on Women, Peace and Security. Previously a policy adviser to Asian governments, in 1994–95 she played a key role in the preparatory process for the Fourth World Conference on Women in Beijing, including organising 1,000 NGOs in the Asia Pacific region to develop the first ever NGO Action Plan. Dr Heyzer has been a founding member of numerous regional and international women's networks and has received several awards for leadership including the Dag Hammarskjöld medal in 2004.

Dr Kamal Hossain (Bangladesh) is a former Minister of Law and former Minister of Foreign Affairs of Bangladesh and is credited with being one of the principal authors of his country's National Constitution. Co-patron (and formerly Chair), of the Commonwealth Human Rights Initiative, and formerly UN Special Rapporteur on Human Rights in Afghanistan, he has recently been highlighting the plight of Afghan refugees and the need for international aid.

Ms Elaine Sihoatani Howard (Tonga) is the Executive Director of Tonga National Youth Congress (Nuku'alofa, Tonga), and Chairperson of the Commonwealth Youth Programme – South Pacific Regional Youth Caucus (RYC) (Honiara, Solomon Islands). She was awarded: *Winner – Best Original Research Presentation* at International Development Conference of New Zealand 2004, and *Overall University Winner,* University of Auckland Postgraduate Research Exposition 2004.

Professor Wangari Muta Maathai (Kenya) is the first African woman to win the Nobel Peace Prize (in 2004). An academic, Professor Maathai's role as an environmental campaigner began in 1977 when she formed an organisation – primarily of women – known as the Green Belt Movement – which mobilised poor women to plant some 30 million trees across Africa. Having been elected to parliament with an overwhelming 98 per cent of the vote in 2002, Professor Wangari Maathai was subsequently appointed by the president as Assistant Minister for Environment, Natural Resources and Wildlife in Kenya's ninth parliament.

The Honourable Ralston Milton Nettleford OM (Jamaica) better known as Rex Nettleford, is a Jamaican scholar, social critic and choreographer. A former Rhodes Scholar he is currently a Vice Chancellor Emeritus of the University of the West Indies where he pursued a first degree in History before proceeding to postgraduate studies at Oxford as a Rhodes Scholar. As a creative artist he founded in 1962 the National Dance Theatre Company of Jamaica, which under his direction has done much to incorporate traditional Jamaican/Caribbean music and movement into a formal balletic repertoire. He is the author of several books including *Mirror Mirror: Identity Race and Protest in Jamaica* and in 1971 compiled, edited, annotated and introduced the speeches and writings of Norman Manley in *Manley and the New Jamaica.* Nettleford established himself as a serious public historian and social critic and was awarded the Order of Merit by the State in recognition of his cultural and scholarly achievements. He was later appointed an ambassador-at-large by his native Jamaica.

HE Mrs Joan Rwabyomere (Uganda) is High Commissioner of Uganda to the UK and Ireland. As a qualified lawyer, she has worked extensively in both business and government. Her positions have included being Vice-Chairman of the Board of Directors, National Enterprises Corporation (1999–2000); Deputy-Director General, External Security (1996–1998); Minister of State for Agriculture (1995–1996); Director, Uganda Electricity Board (1989–1995); Chairman, Board of Directors, Uganda Civil Aviation Authority (1989–1995); Delegate to the EU–ACP Joint Assembly (1989–1995); and a Member of Parliament (1989–1996). Mrs Rwabyomere took up the position of High Commissioner to the UK having been High Commissioner of Uganda to Nigeria from 2001–2005. She has four children.

Mrs Lucy Turnbull (Australia) is an Australian businesswoman and former Lord Mayor of Sydney. For many years she worked as a commercial lawyer and in investment banking. She is a member of the board of the Redfern Waterloo Authority, which was established in 2005 to assist the NSW government to develop a comprehensive plan (social and spatial) for the Redfern–Waterloo area of Sydney, one of the most socio-economically disadvantaged suburbs in Australia. From 1999–2004 she was a member of the Central Sydney Planning Committee. She chairs the Salvation Army Red Shield Appeal in Sydney, and is a member of the Board of Governors of the Woolcock Institute of Medical Research, a respiratory and sleep research institute. She is a board member of Melbourne IT Limited, a publicly listed internet services company, and is a board member of several other private companies in the technology and financial services industries.

Other participants at the meetings

Professor Shamit Saggar, Professor of Political Science, University of Sussex, and Visiting Professor, University of Toronto.

Dr Sarah Ladbury, freelance social development consultant.

Commonwealth Secretariat

Rt Hon Donald McKinnon, Secretary-General

Mrs Florence Mugasha, Deputy Secretary-General

Mr Amitav Banerji, Director, Secretary-General's Office

Mr Matthew Neuhaus, Director, Political Affairs Division

Ms Alexandra Jones, Director, Strategic Planning and Evaluation Division

Ms Daisy Cooper, Planning Officer, Strategic Planning and Evaluation Division

Ms Sabhita Raju, Political Affairs Officer, Good Offices, Political Affairs Division

Appendix B: Written submissions to the Commonwealth Commission on Respect and Understanding

Advisory Board on Naturalisation and Integration, (2007) Submission to the Commission on Integration and Cohesion, re-submitted to the Commonwealth Commission on Respect and Understanding, 12 February, 2007.

Ahmed, Akbar (2007) Submission to the Commonwealth Commission on Respect and Understanding, December 2006.

Gregorios, Archbishop of Thyateira and Great Britain (2007) Submission to the Commonwealth Commission on Respect and Understanding, 7 February, 2007.

Nizami, Farhan (2007) Submission to the Commonwealth Commission on Respect and Understanding, 23 February, 2007.

Office of the Inter Faith Network for the UK (2007) Submission to the Commonwealth Commission on Respect and Understanding, 15 February, 2007.

Premdas, Ralph (2007) 'Multiculturalism as a Policy of Tolerance in the Face of Diversity', submission to the Commonwealth Commission on Respect and Understanding, 16 March, 2007.

Rao, Siriparapu K. (2007) Submission to the Commonwealth Commission on Respect and Understanding, 20 February, 2007.

Royal Commonwealth Society (2007) Submission to the Commonwealth Commission on Respect and Understanding, 16 February, 2007.

Sentamu, John (2007) Submission to the Commonwealth Commission on Respect and Understanding, 22 February, 2007.

The Salvation Army (2007) Submission to the Commonwealth Commission on Respect and Understanding, 12 February, 2007.

Tomlinson, John (2007) 'A Cosmopolitan Perspective'. Submission to the Commonwealth Commission on Respect and Understanding, 8 February, 2007.

Appendix C: Bibliography

Alam, M.Y. and Husband, C., 'British–Pakistani men from Bradford'. Joseph Rowntree Foundation, 2006.

Albro, R., 'The Future of Culture and Rights for Bolivia's Indigenous Movements'. Paper presented at Carnegie Council Fellows Conference, 13–15 June, 2005.

Alderdice, Lord, 'The individual, the group and the psychology of terrorism', *International Review of Psychiatry*, Vol.19 (3), June 2007a.

Alderdice, Lord, 'Introduction, Northern Ireland Assembly Companion - Rulings, Convention and Practice'. Northern Ireland Assembly, TSO Ireland, Belfast, Northern Ireland, 2007b:1–6.

Appiah, K.A., *The Ethics of Identity*, Princeton University Press, Princeton, 2005.

Appiah, K.A., *Cosmopolitanism: Ethics in a World of Strangers*, W.W.Norton & Company, New York, 2006.

Atran, S., 'Global Network Terrorism', Briefing to National Security Council, White House, 28 April, 2006; available at www.sitemaker.umich.edu/satran/files/atran_nsc_042806.pdf and www.au.af.mil/au/awc/awcgate/whitehouse/atrannsc-042806.pdf

Blick, A., Choudhury,T. and Weir, S., *The Rules of the Game. Terrorism, Community and Human Rights*. A report for the Joseph Rowntree Reform Trust by Democratic Audit, Human Rights Centre, University of Essex. Briefing Summary 2007.

Butalia, U., 'Women and Communal Conflict: New Challenges for the Women's Movement in India', in C. Moser and F. Clark (eds) *Victims, Perpetrators or Actors: Gender, Armed Conflict and Political Violence*, Zed Books, London, 2001.

Brighton, S., 'British Muslims, multiculturalism and UK foreign policy: 'integration' and 'cohesion' in and beyond the state', *International Affairs* 83:1, 2007:1–17.

Brown, D., 'A Polyglot of Peoples: Ethnic Diversity and Leadership in the Caribbean Public Sector.' Published in Spanish as 'La Poliglotia de Pueblos: Diversidad Etnica y Liderazgo en el Sector Publico del Caribe', in Oviedo, J. (ed) *Estrategias de Gestion Publica*. Republica Dominicana: Pontificia Universidad Catolica Madre y Maestra, 2004.

Castles, S. and Kosack, G., *Immigrant Workers and Class Structure in Western Europe*, Institute of Race Relations, Oxford University Press, 1973.

Cesari, J., *When Islam and Democracy Meet: Muslims in Europe and the United States*, Palgrave, New York, 2004.

Chaitin, J., 'Stories, Narratives, and Storytelling', in *Beyond Intractability*, Guy Burgess and Heidi Burgess (eds), Conflict Research Consortium, University of Colorado, Boulder, Colorado, USA, July 2003.

Clarke, R. A., *Against All Enemies: Inside America's War on Terror*. Free Press, New York, 2004.

Cohen, A., *Two-Dimensional Man*. Routledge and Kegan Paul, London, 1974.

Control Arms Campaign (Amnesty, Oxfam and IANSA), 'Guns or Growth: Assessing the impact of arms sales on sustainable development'. June 2004

Coussey, M., 'Framework of integration policies', Council of Europe, Strasbourg, 2000.

Cramer, C., *Inequality and Conflict: A Review of an Age-Old Concern*. Identities, Conflict and Cohesion Programme, Paper 11, UNRISD, October, 2005.

Davultoglu, A., *Civilizational Transformation and the Muslim World*. Mahir Publications, Kuala Lumpur, 1994.

Dench, G., Garron, K. and Young, M., *The New East End: Kinship, Race and Conflict*. The Young Foundation, London, 2006.

Eyben, R. and Ladbury, S., 'Building effective states: Taking a citizen's perspective'. Development Research Centre on Citizenship, Participation and Accountability, Institute of Development Studies, University of Sussex, 2006.

Falk, R., 'False universalism and the geopolitics of exclusion: The case of Islam', *Third World Quarterly*, Vol.18, March 1997:7–24.

Fearon, J. and Laitin, D., 'Explaining Interethnic Cooperation', *American Political Science Review*, 1996:715–735.

Friedman, T.L., *Longitudes and Attitudes: Exploring the world after September 11th*. Farrar, Straus and Giroux, New York, 2002.

Fukuyama, F., 'Identity and migration', *Prospect Magazine*, Issue 131, February 2007.

George Washington University Homeland Security Policy Institute and The University of Virginia Critical Incident Analysis Group, 'NETworked Radicalization: A Counter-Strategy', 2007.

Gilley, B., 'Against the concept of ethnic conflict', *Third World Quarterly*, Vol.25, No.6: 1155–1166, 2004.

Harb, M. and Leenders, R., 'Know thy enemy: Hizbullah, "terrorism" and the politics of perception', *Third World Quarterly*, Vol.26, No.1, 2005:173–197.

Heyzer, N., 'Women, War and Peace: Mobilising for Peace and Security in the 21st Century'. The 2004 Dag Hammarskjold Lecture, Uppsala, 2004.

Huntingdon, S.P., *The Clash of Civilizations: And the Remaking of World Order.* Simon and Shuster, New York, 1998.

International Crisis Group, 'Nepal's Maoists: Their Aims, Structure and Strategy'. Asia Report No.104, 27 October, 2005.

Kepel, G., *The War for Muslim Minds: Islam and the West.* The Belknap Press, Cambridge, MA, 2004.

King, R. and Ladbury, S., 'The cultural reconstruction of political reality: Greek and Turkish Cyprus since 1974', *Anthropological Quarterly*, 1984:1–17.

Koh, H. H., (2001) 'Preserving American Values: The challenge at home and abroad', in Strobe Talbott and Nayan Chanda (eds), *The Age of Terror: America and the World after September 11.* Basic Books, New York, 2002.

Lewis, B., 'The Roots of Muslim Rage', *Atlantic Monthly*, September 1990.

Malik, M., 'Discrimination, equality and community cohesion', in *Muslims in the UK: Policies for Engaged Citizens.* Open Society Institute, Budapest, 2005.

Mamdani, M., *Good Muslim, Bad Muslim: America, the Cold War and the Roots of Terror.* Three Leaves Press, Doubleday, New York, 2004.

McGuire, P. and Eyben, K., 'What Now? Reflections report on a political education project with young adults in the rural Loyalist community'. Supported by International Voluntary Service, Northern Ireland, 2004.

Messina, A., *The Logic and Politics of Post-war Immigration.* Cambridge University Press, Cambridge, 2007.

Mirza, M., Senthilkumaran, A. and Ja'far, Z., 'Living apart together – British Muslims and the paradox of multiculturalism'. Policy Exchange, London, 2007.

Nettleford, R., 'The Commonwealth – Reconnection and Renewal: A Voice from the Caribbean', The Commonwealth Lecture, Oxford, 2003.

Open Society Institute, *Monitoring Minority Protection in the EU: The Situation of Muslims in the UK,* EU Monitoring and Advocacy Program (EUMAP), OSI, Budapest, 2002.

Page, B., 'The second death of liberal England', MORI, 2004.

Perera, S., 'The Ethnic Conflict in Sri Lanka: A Historical and Socio-Political Outline'. World Bank, Washington, D.C., 2000.

Putnam, R.D., *Bowling Alone: The Collapse and Revival of American Community.* Simon and Shuster, New York, 2000.

Putzel, J., 'Globalization, liberalization, and prospects for the state', *International Political Science Review,* Vol.26, No.1:5–16, 2005.

Qureshi, A., 'Detention in the Name of the War on Terror: Violations of International Humanitarian and Human Rights Law'. Paper presented at the Bertrand Russell Peace Foundation Conference at the European Parliament on 20 October, 2005.

Ramadan, T., *Western Muslims and the Future of Islam,* Oxford University Press, Oxford, 2004.

Saggar, S., ' Boomerangs and slingshots: radical islamism and counter-terrorism strategy', *Journal of Ethnic and Migration Studies,* forthcoming.

Saggar, S., *Pariah Politics: The Future of Muslim Religious and Political Extremism in Western Democracies,* Oxford University Press, forthcoming.

Sen, A., Human Rights: Is there a Commonwealth Perspective? The first Commonwealth Lecture, London, May, 1998.

Sen, A., 'Global Causes of Violence', Talk given at the Chinese University of Hong Kong in February, 2005.

Sen, A., *Identity and Violence,* Penguin Books, London, 2006.

Sen, A., 'Poverty, War and Peace'. Shortened version of the Nadine Gordimer Lecture given at Wits University and the University of Cape Town, April, 2007.

Slim, H., 'Violent Beliefs'. Paper, The Centre for Humanitarian Dialogue, Geneva, 2005.

Stewart, F., 'Horizontal Inequalities: A neglected dimension of development'. Centre for Research on Inequality Human Security and Ethnicity (CRISE), Working Paper 1. Queen Elizabeth House, University of Oxford, 2004.

Stewart, F., 'Development and Security', Working Paper 3, Centre for Research on Inequality, Human Security and Ethnicity (CRISE), University of Oxford, 2004.

Stewart, F., 'Policies Towards Horizontal Inequalities in Post-Conflict Reconstruction', CRISE Working Paper 7, Queen Elizabeth House, University of Oxford, March, 2005.

Tevoedjre, A., *Winning the War Against Humiliation.* English translation of the Report of the Independent Commission on Africa and the Challenges of the Third Millenium. UNDP, Cotonou, 2003.

Teik, K. B., 'Managing Ethnic Relations in Post-Crisis Malaysia and Indonesia: Lessons from the New Economic Policy?', UNRISD, Geneva, 2004.

Thomas, L., 'Mashing-up Freedom: The Impact of Violence on the Poor in Jamaica'. Paper prepared for UK Department of International Development, London, 2004.

Tomlinson, J., 'Globalization and Cultural Identity'. Keynote paper for Arts and Humanities Research Board Conference, UK, 2003.

Transparency International, 'British Aerospace Systems, Al Yamamah and the UK Serious Fraud Office'. Briefing Note by Transparency International (UK), 15 January, 2006.

Truth & Reconciliation Commission. Available at www.doj.gov.za/trc

UN 'Alliance of Civilizations'. Report of the High-Level Group, 13 November, 2006.

UNDP, *Human Development Report 2005.* 'International cooperation at a crossroads: Aid, trade and security in an unequal world', UNDP, New York, 2005.

Uvin, P., *Aiding Violence.* Kumarian Press, Conneticut, 1998.

Volkan, V., *Killing in the Name of Identity*, Pitchstone Publishing, Virginia, 2006.

Vlachova, M. and Biason, L., (eds), *Women in an Insecure World: Violence Against Women, Facts, Figures and Analysis.* DCAF, Geneva, 2006.

Zunes, S., 'Political Islam: Revealing the Roots of Extremism'. Centre for Policy Analysis on Palestine, 2005.

Selected Commonwealth and other agency publications

Commonwealth Foundation, 'Citizens and Goverance Toolkit', 2004.

Commonwealth Youth Programme, Strategic Plan, 2006–2008.

'Making Democracy Work for Pro-poor Development'. Report of the Commonwealth Expert Group on Development and Democracy, Commonwealth Secretariat, London, 2003:43.

'Speaking up for small states', in *Development and Democracy: Report of the Commonwealth Secretary General, 2003.*

'Social Dimensions of International Migration'. Third Coordination Meeting on International Migration, Department of Economic and Social Affairs, UN, 2004:2.

Rao, S.K., 'Poverty, Democracy and Development. Issues for Consideration by the Commonwealth Expert Group on Democracy and Development', Commonwealth Secretariat, London, 2004.